ON SOME BOOKS BY EILEEN R. TABIOS

Reproductions of the Empty Flagpole

... exposes Tabios's search through history and art to understand her central demands—to perceive freely, to investigate color, to be a fully responsive being. "Can you pay the price for risking perception and imperceptibility?" she asks in "The Continuance of the Gaze," and then answers, "I trust in radiance. Let: Us." —*Publishers Weekly*

Hiraeth: Tercets from the Last Archipelago

"For pure line-by-line loveliness, Eileen Tabios's *Hiraeth* sates my thirst for intelligence." —Minal Hajratwala, *Poetry* (Editors' Blog)

The In(ter)vention of the Hay(na)ku: Selected Tercets 1996-2019

Too many readers overlook a poem's form, ironically. Tabios does not. Yet she's always bending it. // James Joyce found poetry too confining. Tabios must always transcend her own formalisms—their own magnitude and brilliance. // I'm awed by her intellect that's always understated. —Burt Kimmelman, *Marsh Hawk Review*

The Light Sang As It Left Your Eyes: Our Autobiography

The Light Sang documents a restlessness, an ardent quest for a means of pure saying, for a methodology of comprehending both one's self in the world and the world within one's self. —Fred Muratori, *American Book Review*

Since American Confessionalism and the British Movement, there's been a steady attempt to reclaim autobiographical writing in the cause of an ever more "innovative" poetics. The contentious term of "radical autobiography" has thus been evolving—from the earliest orientations of the New York School through to early and current Language writings—in a consistent if at times calculated way. // Tabios' *The Light* . . . does not easily situate itself within one of these competing camps, but rather seems to accomplish the feat of making poetic diversity a value in itself. // Death, and silence, is the distillation of complexity and diversity, of all these vibrant languages, forms and histories, into something which unites them. It is perfection, yet such is Eileen Tabios' vitalizing disposition, that even this perfection cannot seem an end. It too becomes poetic affirmation: *"Don't ever stop. Be mad with me. Be ecstasy. Be me . . ."* —Nicholas Manning, *Cordite*

The Opposite of Claustrophia: Prime's Anti-Autobiography

The title of this experimental poetry collection references the inventive approach Eileen R. Tabios took to write . . . poems that Eric Gamalinda calls "an incantatory catalogue that is spiritually tethered to the body and the earth." Tabios' technique is unique and "startling—not just for the method but for the lines of breathtaking beauty . . ." —*New York Magazine*

I Take Thee, English, for My Beloved

In his "Discourse in the novel" Mikhail M. Bakhtin writes: "The poet must assume a complete single-personed hegemony over his own language, he must assume equal responsibility for each one of its aspects and subordinate them to his own, and only his own, intentions. Each word must express the poet's meaning directly and without mediation: there must be no distance between the poet and his word. . . . To achieve this, the poet strips the word of others' intentions, he uses only such words and forms (and only in such a way) that they lose their link with concrete intentional levels of language and their connection with specific contexts." // Bakhtin's description of the poet approaches Eileen Tabios's active involvement. *I Take Thee, English, for My Beloved* is a phantasmagoric journey of 504 pages into one of the most interesting embodiments of contemporary poetry.

—Anny Ballardini, *Jacket*

Ménage à Trois with the 21st Century

There are times I am reminded of Olson: how he took Maximus of Tyre as his spiritual-poetic mentor, placing him in the Gloucester of the 20th century. Eileen's circumstance is not too dissimilar. Where the two differ is in the messages they both 'receive' from their respective muse, and then 'translate' that message to us the reader . . . Eileen differs in her approach. We come to know her mind in a more intimate, compassionate way. She probes with depth and questions her surroundings, relating them back to her ancient muse, thereby placing Enheduanna in the present day. She seems at times to be entranced, totally absorbed in 'otherness'. This 'experience' . . . assumes the nature of a mystical/transcendent phenomenon.

—Ric Carfagna, *Poetic Inhalation*

147 Million Orphans (MMXI-MML)

The book amounts to a powerful (and polyvocal) meditation on orphanhood, adoption, education, the poetics of language acquisition, and multiple authorship . . . lyrically intense and structurally adventurous.

—Michael Leong, *Stalactite Chandelier*

Dredging for Atlantis

Jack Kerouac wrote, "Vision is deception." Eileen Tabios' version goes like this: "Go forth and prettily miscalculate."

—Jeffrey Cyphers Wright, *The Brooklyn Rail*

. . . many [poems] contained a startling turn of phrase that invited deeper contemplation, an effect I crave and the reason why I read poetry. Others just made me wonder what Tabios was smoking.

—Vita Foster, *The Feminist Review*

The Secret Lives of Punctuations, Vol. 1

A critique of presumptions of transparent referentiality and unproblematic narrative—coupled with the pleasure of stretching the imagination with formal innovations—has been an important feature of all of Tabios's poetry."

—Thomas Fink, *Jacket*

Because I Love You, I Become War

Tabios was the first Filipino American poet that I read and actually liked. I often compare other poets to American or British poets that I had read in college or during the time I was re-discovering poetry. It would be unfair to compare Tabios to anyone else other than herself.

—Eunice Barbara C. Novio, *Inquirer.net*

Nota Bene Eiswein

Tabios takes the reader to an imaginative height the reader could not have anticipated at the poem's beginning.

—Grace Ocasio, *Jacket*

Post Bling Bling

Olson and Tabios recognize the mythic substratum that exists beneath our imagination of this "stuff," whether it is constructed of fructose, image, phosphate, plastic, or language.

—Garin Cycholl, *Rain Taxi*

THE INVENTOR

PREVIOUSLY BY EILEEN R. TABIOS

POETRY

After The Egyptians Determined the Shape of the World is A Circle, 1996

Beyond Life Sentences, 1998

The Empty Flagpole (CD with guest artist Mei-mei Berssenbrugge), 2000

Ecstatic Mutations (with short stories and essays), 2001

Reproductions of the Empty Flagpole, 2002

Enheduanna in the 21st Century, 2002

There, Where the Pages Would End, 2003

Menage a Trois With the 21st Century, 2004

Crucial Bliss Epilogues, 2004

The Estrus Gaze(s), 2005

Songs of the Colon, 2005

Post Bling Bling, 2005

I Take Thee, English, For My Beloved, 2005

The Secret Lives of Punctuations, Vol. I, 2006

Dredging for Atlantis, 2006

It's Curtains, 2006

Silences: The Autobiography of Loss, 2007

The Singer and Others: Flamenco Hay(na)ku, 2007

The Light Sang As It Left Your Eyes: Our Autobiography, 2007

Nota Bene Eiswein, 2009

Footnotes to Algebra: Uncollected Poems 1995-2009, 2009

On A Pyre: An Ars Poetica, 2010

Roman Holiday, 2010

Hay(na)ku for Haiti, 2010

The Thorn Rosary: Selected Prose Poems and New 1998-2010, 2010

the relational elations of Orphaned Algebra (with j/j hastain), 2012

5 Shades of Gray, 2012

The Awakening: A Long Poem Triptych & A Poetics Fragment, 2013

147 Million Orphans (MMXI-MML), 2014

44 Resurrections, 2014

Sun Stigmata (Sculpture Poems), 2014

I Forgot Light Burns, 2015

Duende in the Alleys, 2015

Invent(st)ory: Selected Catalog Poems & New (1996-2015), 2015

The Connoisseur of Alleys, 2016

The Gilded Age of Kickstarters, 2016

Excavating the Filipino in Me, 2016

I Forgot Ars Poetica, 2016

Amnesia: Somebody's Memoir, 2016

The Opposite of Claustrophobia: Prime's Anti-Autobiography, 2017

Post-Ecstasy Mutations, 2017

On Green Lawn, The Scent of White, 2017

To Be an Empire Is to Burn, 2017

If They Hadn't Worn White Hoods . . . (with John Bloomberg-Rissman), 2017

What Shivering Monks Comprehend, 2017

Your Father Is Bald: Selected Hay(na)ku Poems, 2017

Immigrant: Hay(na)ku & Other Poems In A New Land, 2017

Comprehending Mortality (with John Bloomberg-Rissman), 2017

Big City Cante Intermedio, 2017

Winter on Wall Street: A Novella-in-Verse, 2017

Making National Poetry Month Great Again, 2017

Manhattan: An Archaeology, 2017

Love In A Time of Belligerence, 2017

Murder Death Resurrection: A Poetry Generator, 2018

Tanka, Vol. I, 2018

Hiraeth: Tercets From The Last Archipelago, 2018

One, Two, Three: Selected Hay(na)ku Poems (Trans. Rebeka Lembo), 2018

The Great American Novel: Selected Visual Poetry 2001-2019, 2019

The In(ter)vention of the Hay(na)ku: Selected Tercets 1996-2019, 2019 & 2021

Witness in the Convex Mirror, 2019

Evocare: Selected Tankas (with Ayo Gutierrez and Brian Cain Anne), 2019

We Are It, 2020

Inculpatory Evidence: The Covid-19 Poems, 2020

Political Love, 2021

La Vie érotique de l'art, une séance avec William Carlos Williams (Trad. de l'anglais (États-Unis) par Samuel Rochery), 2021

Prises (Trad. de l'anglais (États-Unis) par Fanny Garin), 2022

Because I Love You, I Become War, 2023

FICTION

Behind the Blue Canvas, 2004

Novel Chatelaine, 2009

Silk Egg: Collected Novels 2009-2009, 2011

What Counts, 2020

Pagpag: The Dictator's Aftermath in the Diaspora, 2020

Dovelion: A Fairy Tale for Our Times, 2021

Simmering: a novella-in-prose-poems, 2022

Getting to One, flash fictions with art by harry k stammer, 2023

PROSE COLLECTIONS

Black Lightning: Poetry-In-Progress (poetry essays/interviews), 1998

My Romance (art essays with poems), 2002

The Blind Chatelaine's Keys (biography with haybun), 2008

Against Misanthropy: A Life in Poetry (2015-1995), 2015

#EileenWritesNovel, 2017

Tiny Stickers: A Covid-19 Autobiography, 2020

Kapwa's Novels, 2022

The Inventor: A Poet's Transcolonial Autobiography, 2023

THE INVENTOR

A Poet's Transcolonial Autobiography

Eileen R. Tabios

MARSH HAWK PRESS · 2023

EAST ROCKAWAY, NEW YORK

Marsh Hawk books are published by Marsh Hawk Press, Inc.,
a not-for-profit corporation under section 501(c)3
United States Internal Revenue Code.

Cover art: *Anghelpugay ng Kasarinlan (Elegiac Angel of Independence)*, 1998, acrylic on canvas
scroll (approx. 3' × 7') by Jose Tence Ruiz who created it to commemorate the Centennial
Anniversary of the Philippines' June 12, 1898 Declaration of Independence from Spain.
Cover design: Mark Melnick
Interior design & typesetting: Mark Melnick

FIRST EDITION
Library of Congress Cataloging-in-Publication Data
Names: Tabios, Eileen, author.
Title: The inventor : a poet's transcolonial autobiography / Eileen R. Tabios.
Description: East Rockaway, New York : Marsh Hawk Press, 2023. |
Includes bibliographical references and index. |
Identifiers: LCCN 2023021602 | ISBN 9781732614192 (paperback)
Subjects: LCSH: Tabios, Eileen. | Filipino American authors--Biography |
American poetry--Filipino American authors--History and criticism. | Poetics.
Classification: LCC PS3570.A234 Z46 2023 | DDC 811/.54--dc23/eng/20230606
LC record available at https://lccn.loc.gov/2023021602

Publication of this title was made possible in part by a regrant awarded
and administered by the Community of Literary Magazines and Presses (CLMP).
CLMP's NYS regrant programs are made possible by the New York State Council on
the Arts with the support of Governor Kathy Hochul and the New York State Legislature.

Marsh Hawk Press
P.O. Box 206, East Rockaway, N.Y. 11518-0206
mheditor@marshhawkpress.org

Contents

IN ORDER TO BECOME A POET

This is who I am. I loved journalism. I spent my high school and college years working towards my goal of winning a Pulitzer Prize for excellent reportage. After college, I worked in an entry position at *The New York Times* with other news clerks who eventually received that Pulitzer (such as Susan Faludi). But I fell in love and lost myself in that love. No need to belabor that story, except to say that it caused me to disregard my job and eventually move on to a new career.

Since I covered financial news at the end of my journalism career, I entered the finance industry and later worked for three of the world's biggest banks representing Britain, Japan, and Switzerland. As I would joke ten years later after switching "careers" one more time to become a poet, I thought I had to become a banker in order to become a poet because that's what T.S. Eliot did.

I referenced Eliot's banking background several times during my early years as a poet. I knew it was because I felt uneasy with other poets learning about my finance or non-literary background. My worries ceased when I mentioned that anxiety to the poet with whom I spent much of my first summer in San Francisco after moving there from New York City. He firmly replied, "I don't judge poets by how they make money. There is no one way to be a poet." Since that poet was Philip Lamantia who helped shape the Surrealist and Beat movements in the United States, I knew he knew of what he spoke. *There is no one way to be a poet.*

A PERSONAL INTRODUCTION

My first book was of poetry and contained no words.

I also wrote it when I was about two or three years old, but that first book was a harbinger to what would become my poet's life: my poetry is not my words.

I was born in 1960 in a country that was among the United States' first colonies: the Philippines. As a result of the U.S.' forays beyond North America for expanding its empire, English became the predominant language across the Philippine archipelago, becoming speech for politics, commerce, and education. As soon as I entered school, I was introduced to English so that, as a 10-year-old immigrant to the United States, language was not a barrier to assimilating into my new country.

My mother, Beatriz Tilan Tabios, was an elementary school teacher at Brent School, itself a colonial legacy as it educated the children of U.S.-American military, missionaries, and mining prospectors stationed in the Philippines. My father, Filamore Tabios, Sr., taught accounting at the local Baguio University in addition to working as a businessman. They raised their children to appreciate reading, with numerous volumes of *Encyclopedia Brittanica* dominating my memory of our living room's bookshelves. My brothers favored science fiction and comics. For the latter, you could rent-to-read comics for a few centavos with patrons standing in or just outside the stores to read. Since my parents didn't allow me to patronize those shops, I mostly read *Grimms' Fairy Tales* and Homer's *The Odyssey* at home. When I passed by those comic book stalls, some of their male contingent would hoot out a paradoxical compliment for being another colonial insult, "White legs! White legs!" I would glare even as I envied them: *how I wish I could read what they were reading!*

Colonialism affected curriculum so that, during World War II, my mother's family occasionally fled to the mountains to avoid Japanese soldiers visiting their village, Mama would pack a Shakespeare volume along with a small bag of rice. While the rice was to lessen the stress of meals their mountain hosts would have to provide, Shakespeare was to feed my bibliophile mother in a different way. As a student, she'd also memorized William Ernest Henley's 1875 poem "Invictus," so that she came to recite it out loud decades later when we watched the 2009 Clint Eastwood-directed "Invictus," to the appreciation of the movie audience who might otherwise have shushed those talking out loud.

In 1970, newly arrived in the United States, reading became my haven as I proved to be unpopular in elementary school after a first school day of being inspected as a new immigrant student. *I hid amidst sentences and paragraphs—I hid in words.* Steeped in words, my first career became journalism. I wasn't thinking of journalism as a goal when I joined the staff of my middle school's magazine. But that initial exposure solidified my love for words, even as I couldn't imagine manifesting that love through other means like creative writing. I focused on journalism because news reporting offered the benefit of taking me out of my introspection—I was a shy child—to deal with the outside world for covering its news. In Gardena, located in the South Bay region of Los Angeles County, I became the editor of my high school newspaper, Gardena High's *Smoke Signals*, as well as the high school correspondent for the local paper, *Gardena Valley News*. When I attended Barnard College, I joined the staff of *Spectator*, Columbia University's daily newspaper and eventually became its News Editor. After college, my first job was an entry position at *The New York Times*.

As a journalist, I was trained by those who covered news before the advent of "New Journalism," a style of news writing developed in the 1960s and 1970s that's characterized by a subjective perspective—of reporters immersing themselves or their opinions into their stories. On the other hand, I was trained to cover matters "objectively"—I'll never forget a crusty, old male editor gruffly reminding me, *Just the facts, Ma'am!* I still believe journalists should attempt to be objective, even though I know it can be impossible—as poetry reveals, it's impossible to get away from one's "I."

I loved journalism. I spent my high school and college years working towards my goal of winning a Pulitzer Prize for excellent reportage. After college, I worked in an entry position at *The New York Times* with other news clerks who eventually received that Pulitzer (such as Susan

Faludi and Alix Freedman). But I fell in love and lost myself in that love. No need to belabor that story, except to say that it caused me to disregard my job and eventually move on to a new career. Since I was covering financial news towards the end of my journalism career, I entered the finance industry and later worked for three of the world's biggest banks representing Britain, Japan, and Switzerland. As I would joke ten years later after switching "careers" one more time to become a poet, I thought I had to become a banker in order to become a poet because that's what T.S. Eliot did.

I returned to writing when, in entering what became the last two years of my banking career, I recalled my old dreams. I didn't want to return to journalism since that seemed pointless. But in feeling my love for words, I decided to write a novel—the so-called Great American Novel—in the evenings after my banking hours. I resigned from banking after I put "The End" to the novel's first draft. Since my last banking day was a June 30, I thought I'd take the summer off from work—I was exhausted from a finance career that required longer hours than the stereotyped 9 to 5. I thought to return to the novel in the fall. Meanwhile, to recover from my finance career, I thought I'd write in a shorter form than the novel and thought of poems.

At that point, I hadn't paid much attention to poetry; the only youthful involvement I recall with poetry was some elementary school activity of memorizing long poems for a competition that I did not win. That post-banking summer, I learned poetry from scratch by reading almost all the poetry collections in my neighborhood's Barnes & Noble bookstore. While reading, I also wrote poems. As a result of that immersion, after summer ended and I was supposed to return to my novel, I realized that poetry was the form I'd been looking for as a writer. I had felt something *pure* about words from keeping company with poems—pure in the sense that words seem to bear certain characteristics that create their own nature versus the utilitarian purpose(s) for which humans used them. I felt a deep urge to know words more fully than as the communications medium required by journalism or financial research papers. Poet-biographer Richard Perceval Graves (and other poets) posit, "poets are born, not made." If so, I'd be an example of Graves' "general rule." I immediately felt a *rightness* to working as a poet, as if I'd finally found the right role for relating with words, a role that I once thought was fulfilled by journalism.

That hot New York summer, thus, turned my primary focus away from fiction to poetry. As for that novel, I later read it with fresh eyes and objectively—or as a reader versus its author—understood it to be crap. It was a murder mystery set in a bank—how tediously predictable. I've since lost track of the manuscript's whereabouts, but I am grateful to it, not for any literary merit but for getting me out of banking and into poetry.

Newly committed to poetry, I began considering aspects of my raw material of language and remembered how English entered my birthland as a colonizing tool. When I came across Nick Carbo's edited anthology of Filipino and Filipino American poets, I was jolted by the empathy and recognition I felt for its title: *Returning the Borrowed Tongue* (1996). The "borrowed tongue" refers to Filipinos becoming fluent in their colonizer's language. The phrase is also a euphemism since "enforced tongue" would be more accurate. I then understood that, as a poet, I didn't want to write in this inherited English. Writing well is the best revenge, according to many writers including some Filipino poets, but it wasn't enough for me to master its grammar and possess a wide vocabulary. I wanted to upend English itself by disrupting its dictionary definitions, disputing its structures, and however else I could concoct. It's synchronistic that my "first book" can be categorized as visual poetry, itself a category that questions normative genres by second-guessing text's primacy through visual imagery.

What I didn't realize until much later was that politics, though significant, was not the true nature of what I aspired to do as a poet. My accent is Filipino but what I was learning was to evolve from English as a tool for communications because to colonize, too, is to communicate, as in communicate the colonizer's desires. What I was learning was to evolve from English towards the language of Poetry.

Poetry, for me, is a language that transcends genre or dictionary definitions. I realize I understood this at birth, as shown by my first "book." It bore no title. It was created by my toddler-self folding a piece of paper to emulate a book's pages. The first page bore a green Crayola scrawl at the bottom of the page. The second page bore a yellow Crayola circle at the top right corner of the page. The third page bore a brown Crayola scrawl at the bottom of the page. But those childish images clearly contained meaning akin to what would be found in text. It could be considered visual and asemic poetries. The "text" of its three pages might be interpreted as follows:

The grass is green.

The sun is out shining.

The sun burnt the grass.

From that start of upending English into Poetry so that its words became visual, I began writing poems characterized as "abstract," "surreal," and "fragmented." A lover of the visual arts, I also sought inspiration in that medium to look away from literary traditions. Abstract expressionism was useful for creating prose poems because its form avoided line-breaks that might interrupt the energy flow within my lines; in addition, it helped me conceptualize deleting the period at the end of the prose poem's last sentence to symbolize how the poem continues past the end of words, in the same way abstract expressionist brushstrokes seemingly continue past the edge of a canvas. My first U.S.-published poetry book is a collection of such prose poems: *Reproductions of the Empty Flagpole* (2002); *Reproductions* also reprinted the prose poems that appeared in my first poetry book, *Beyond Life Sentences* (1998) which was released in the Philippines and received its National Book Award for Poetry (from the Manila Critics Circle). Later, emulating sculptors—specifically Michelangelo carving out the Renaissance masterpiece "David" from a block of marble—I returned to those prose poems and chiseled out new verses from its paragraph-blocks of words to create a new book, *Sun Stigmata* (2014).

I didn't leave fiction entirely. There, my rambunctious disputations of literary norms included entitling a book *The Great American Novel* (2019) for a collection of visual poetry. I created a compilation of seven-chapter novels, *Silk Egg* (2011), which could be considered prose poems instead of short novels. Recently, I finished my second novel, *Collateral Damage*, by arbitrarily collaging one-paragraph prose poems as the first paragraphs in all its chapters; these poems had not been written to develop the novel's plot and would have no connection to developing the novel's story, except for what the reader may read into them. *Collateral Damage* reflects my radical trust in, and desire to maximize the agency of, the reader.

Eventually, I moved towards inventing new poetry forms, and created the "hay(na)ku." Its name is derived after a common Filipino expression "hay naku" or "ay naku," which is akin to the English "Oh!" or "Oh my

gosh!" and whose meaning depends on context. For examples, a lover
might say, "Hay naku—your skin is so soft I just want to caress you" or
a mother might yell to misbehaving children, "Hay naku! Stop scream-
ing and get your butts over here!" I appreciated how the meaning of
words need not be fixed, fluctuating due to different contexts. Such flux
in meaning affirms my view that a poem's reception differs per reader
and can't be controlled by the poet.

Equally significant, with the hay(na)ku I was able to create poetry by
offering other poets a form in which to write. The hay(na)ku is a tercet,
with the first line being one word, the second line being two words, and
the third line being three words. By creating a form, it was up to others
to use words to flesh out that form into poems. The hay(na)ku came to
travel around the world with poets I could not have envisioned would
be interested. Many were unknown to me, with some living in countries
I've never visited, such as Macedonia, Finland, Australia, among others.
For me, helping to create new poems with others' words, not mine, befits
how Poetry as a language is the opposite of colonialism: it is a language
of community. Instead of being a language of authority (e.g., authorial
authority), control, and exclusion, Poetry is a language for openness,
acceptance, and inclusion. Poetry, thus, is already a decolonized lan-
guage. *How freeing I have found Poetry to be!*

Chapter 2

THE HAY(NA)KU

Poetry is the tree that did not fall if there was no one in the forest to see or hear it drop. Without a respondent, (my) poetry doesn't exist—that verse merely would be a static compilation of words.

I began the previous chapter by offering how *my poetry is not my words*. I differentiate between the terms "poetry" and "poem" in the way I differentiate between a movie and a snapshot. I consider the poem a snapshot. But the way a poem was formed through something happening with the poet and later responded to by its reader or audience is, for me, a movie. That movie requires another or others to form an audience. Readers will be the ones to make meaning from poems. In that experience instigated by my poems, that movie ideally would not just generate a reader interpretation that I did not anticipate, but also end in some beneficial action. For example, if I wrote a poem castigating a dictator—and I've written plenty about the Philippine Martial Law dictator Ferdinand Marcos, Sr.—perhaps its reader would be moved to question history texts that elide Martial Law abuses (such texts exist as Marcos' supporters attempted to re-write history). Or, if I wrote a poem decrying environmental damage, perhaps its reader might be moved to behave more responsibly to protect the environment.

From the beginning of writing poems, I felt the importance of reader response—I empathize with "reader-response theory" which argues that a text has no meaning before a reader experiences or reads it. One of my favorite poetic series is comprised of "Footnote Poems" from my book, *I Take Thee, English, For My Beloved* (2005). Each poem's text is 1-3 lines and printed at the bottom of an otherwise blank page. The reader is asked to imagine—if not actually write on the predominantly blank page—what might have generated the footnote. I designed the format to give space to readers since the footnote poems (like all poems) are open to varied responses. Here's a monostich example that could generate numerous and different stories:

He still believed she would save him from entanglement with
memory's underbrush.

Privileging the reader(s)' role fit with how community formation, or community, addressed my reluctance to be in a language that helped colonize others. The hay(na)ku became a metaphor for disrupting the colonizer's desire to control others and, instead, allowing others to propound their views. It felt logical to push this outward-looking perspective into relying more on the reader-poet versus author to create poems, thus, the hay(na)ku which is a poetic form but not a poem itself. With hindsight, it's fitting that I even agreed for someone else to name my invention: Vince Gotera who suggested "hay(na)ku." Moreover, while the hay(na)ku originated as a single tercet, unlike with most poetry forms, the hay(na)ku encourages variations, including radical ones, from its readers. Indeed, the number of variations known to me numbered over 20 in the first year after the form's release to the public and were mostly created by other poets and artists (a variation by Charles Bernstein, "Ku(na)hay," appears in *The Best American Poetry*, 2008). The hay(na)ku also evolved to accommodate other disciplines such as visual art, theater, and comics.

· · ·

Origin

In 2000, I began a "Counting Journal" with the idea that counting would be, as I wrote in that journal, "another mechanism for me to understand my days." I intended to do so by counting everything countable within my daily life. For example, on December 18, 2000, I wrote:

> *Bush secured Electoral College majority—271 votes—*
> *to become the U.S.' 43rd President. It was announced*
> *that Hillary Clinton received an $8.0 mio. advance for*
> *a memoir for her years in the White House. With Simon*
> *and Schuster. So much $ for gossip when one can't even*
> *find the more modest sum to publish a poetry book!*

My Counting Journal was inspired, as its first entry explained on Sept. 20, 2000, by Ianthe Brautigan's *You Can't Catch Death—A Daughter's*

Memoir. In the memoir, she mentions the boy Cameron in her father Richard Brautigan's novel, *The Hawkline Monster*: "Cameron was a counter. He vomited nineteen times to San Francisco. He liked to count everything."

The character Cameron came to impress me when my Counting Journal lasted for only five months because I could maintain its underlying obsession for only that long. But it included a January 18, 2001 entry that birthed the hay(na)ku:

> *On plane returning to San Francisco, read* Selected Letters
> of Jack Kerouac. *P. 46—Kerouac says, "I think American*
> *haikus should never have more than 3 words in a line—e.g.*

> *Trees can't reach*
> *for a glass*
> *of water*

I included Kerouac's notion of an "American haiku" because of its reference of a count ("no more than 3 words in a line"). But its concept must have lingered deep in my mind since, later, I posted an announcement on Flips, a listserv of Filipino writers or anyone interested in Filipino literature that was co-founded by poets Nick Carbo and Vince Gotera. After referencing Kerouac and his notion of American haiku, I stated:

> *I am inaugurating the Filipino Haiku! Pinoy Poets:*
> *Attention! I'll post if you send me some: 3 lines each*
> *having one, two, three words in order—e.g.*

> *Trees*
> *can't reach*
> *for a glass*

Filipino or Pinoy poets responded with enthusiasm partly because, as Michelle Bautista noted, the idea of one-two-three "works with the Filipino nursery rhyme: *isa, dalawa, tatlo, ang tatay mo'y kalbo* (pronounce phonetically to catch the rhythm). The rhyme amusingly translates into English as "one, two, three: your dad is bald."

Here are two hay(na)ku by Oliver de la Paz:

Keats
writes darkly.
Birds trill unseen.

.

Watches
around wrists
make teeth marks.

Here's another by Patrick Rosal:

NYC PINOY BLUES OR
THE AY NAKU HAIKU

God-
damn—same
shit / different dog

In these and other works, what's evident is that the charge associated with the haiku also can be present in the Pinoy form with the type of paradox that one might find in the Filipino *bagoong*—a pungent fish sauce enjoyed by Filipinos but, ahem, misunderstood by non-Filipinos. Thus, did Catalina Cariaga also offer:

onion
just eaten;
smell my breath

At the time of conceptualizing the hay(na)ku, I was mostly focused on the prose poem form and considered myself a maximalist rather than the minimalist who would have more affinity with short poetry forms. I was amused at what I considered poetry's sense of humor—that a textually verbose poet like me would create such a condensed form. But I appreciated the result as many poets wrote what I considered better poems than I could achieve in hay(na)ku. In other words, poets wrote those wonderful poems because I presented a reason for them to do so. I thought, *What an effective way to be a poet!*

While I mostly considered my hay(na)ku only average, I did pen one tercet that pleased me enough to become my go-to single-tercet example of my hay(na)ku:

Blueness
of sky—
I am breathing

At its introduction, the form was not yet called hay(na)ku, but Filipino Haiku or Pinoy Haiku. While the Flips listserv's poets enthusiastically penned what Vince Gotera called "Stairstep Tercets," my project also created a discussion on the implications of *Naming*—and how I was approaching it by using the phrase "Pinoy Haiku." Vince asked:

> *Appropriating the "haiku" name has all sorts of prosodic and*
> *postcolonial problems (by which I mean the WWII "colonizing"*
> *of the Philippines by Japan, among other things). Am I being*
> *overly serious here? When you say Kerouac refers to "American*
> *haiku" not having more than three words per line, I think*
> *he might have been reacting to Allen Ginsberg's "American*
> *sentence," which has 17 syllables per line. I guess my concern*
> *about calling it a "Pinoy haiku" is that readers could say,*
> *"Hey, Pinoys can't even get the haiku right!" They won't always*
> *have the Kerouac quote to guide them. Besides, why must we*
> *always be doing things in reaction to the term "American"?*
> *An interesting parallel poetic-form-naming might be Baraka's*
> *"low coup" form (the diametrical opposite of "high coup" /*
> *haiku). Maybe the Pinoy version could be the "hay (na)ku"?*

Another poet suggested that I also rename the project because the traditional haiku form should be respected. Well, yes and no. As I told that poet—I think that, in Poetry, rules are sometimes made to be broken.

Also, I initially wasn't moved by Vince's notion as regards Japan "colonizing" the Philippines during World War II. If anything, I thought that were I to consider that line of thinking (which I hadn't been), I didn't mind subverting the Japanese haiku form specifically because it could be considered as *talking back* against Japanese imperialism. Still, upon closer consideration, I realized that the perspective could work both ways, and that using the "haiku" reference could imply a continuation of "colonial mentality."

Ultimately, I bowed to Vince's wisdom and renamed the form "hay(na) ku." I also appreciated the implications of inventing something but giving up the naming to someone else. In addition to hay(na)ku being a better name, I wanted my release of naming rights to symbolize the opposite of authorial control, a kind of control a colonizer would exercise.

Later, I also realized that I didn't wish to reference haiku because of its focus on syllables and how the syllabic note might relate to music. It's been said by many that *poetry should sing*, but that's a statement I've long thought to be reductive. I don't believe poetic music can be defined, thus supporting my preference for words over syllables in poetry—I liked how the hay(na)ku's word can be one to 18 syllables (if "pneumonoultramicroscopicsilicovolcanoconiosis" is the longest English word, at least as determined by Oxford dictionaries which define it as "a lung disease caused by inhaling very fine ash and sand dust"). I prefer words because it takes words, not syllables, for me to think (although one need not make the choice and perhaps other poets can argue persuasively that a syllable can think). I don't feel poetry should sing so much as it should think. In poetry (unlike perhaps elsewhere), thinking is not the opposite of music and, indeed, concepts can sing.

. . .

The Hay(na)ku Grows and Spreads

On Flips, enough Filipino poets responded warmly to hay(na)ku so that I was encouraged to introduce the form to others. I presented it in 2003 to the larger world on Philippine Independence Day, or June 12, as a call for poems, many of which would form *The First Hay(na)ku Anthology* coedited by Flips member Jean Vengua and Australia-based poet Mark Young (2005). I chose Philippine Independence Day because of my desire to expand English or U.S.-American poetry with a Filipino form or, as I specifically considered it, a "Filipino diasporic form." I was affected by knowing how, in the United States, Filipino-Americans have often been ignored or subsumed into larger "Asian American" contexts and I wanted to center Filipinos.

Related to such disregard, Independence Day for the Philippines was originally July 4 to mimic the U.S.-American holiday before it was changed to June 12, the anniversary of the Philippines' 1898 Declaration of Independence from Spain. Neither Spain or the United States recognized Philippine sovereignty and Spain later ceded the Philippines to the U.S. through the 1898 Treaty of Paris. The Philippines refused to recognize the treaty, and the bloody Philippine-American War began. With the U.S.' military might, the Philippines lost the war to become a U.S. colony. The U.S. granted independence on July 4, 1946, a date chosen for corresponding to the U.S. Independence Day.

By announcing the hay(na)ku on June 12, I wanted to hearken the authentic Philippine Independence Day—the symbol might not be obvious to those unfamiliar with Philippine history, but it was important to me for affirming why I wanted to create a Filipino diasporic poetry form. I wanted to not just inherit English but adjust it, in this case, expanding (English) poetry's expanse by hearkening Philippine history—for instance, if a poet was to write a hay(na)ku, that poet inevitably would wonder what the word means. The questioning would bring attention to Filipino language and perhaps Filipino history and culture.

Since the public release of the hay(na)ku, a hay(na)ku contest was judged by Barbara Jane Reyes which was popular in the internet's poetry blogland; the hay(na)ku form was taught by Junichi P. Semitsu, then Director of "June Jordan's Poetry for the People" program at the African American Studies Department at U.C. Berkeley; Mexican poet Ernesto Priego wrote the first hay(na)ku book, *Not Even Dogs* (2006); the hay(na)ku spread to the visual poetry and visual art worlds; and many poets and visual artists around the world—non-Filipino as well as Filipino—picked up the form to write it as I originally conceived as well as to offer variations. By 2018 (which was when I ceased meticulously tracking its publications), the hay(na)ku appeared in numerous literary journals and about 80 single-author poetry collections: the latter includes 12 dedicated only to the hay(na)ku, including an all-Finnish hay(na)ku book by Heikki Lahnaoja. In 2017, I released in Romania the trilingual limited edition *Your Father Is Bald*, which presents some of my hay(na)ku in English with Romanian and Spanish translations. The form also has generated several anthologies edited by six different editors that presented the hay(na)ku as text, as collaborations, as visual art or visual poetry, and as comic strips. I even had the pleasure of judging a hay(na)ku poetry contest coordinated by Elizabeth Johnston for Canada's Festival de l'Ail de Ste-Anne Garlic Festival. The winning tercet is by Sheila Murphy—

Monsoon
flavored Arizona
mojo de Ajo

which I praised in my Judge's Statement for "its clever layers involv-
ing synesthetic volta with a culinary metaphor. A monsoon is unlikely to
reach the desert that is much of Arizona. But a rainstorm, and (as sug-
gested) one that's a side-effect of a far-away monsoon, might touch this
U.S. state—it just 'flavors' Arizona. In such case, that rainstorm might
be as welcome as a mojo de Ajo—or garlic gravy—that improves (if not
rescues) a dry side of beef. Of course, the steak need not be desert-like
and mojo de Ajo still can elevate a perfectly turned-out dish, whether it's
steak, chicken, shrimp, pasta or popcorn."

More recently, in June 2023, writer Malou Alorro taught the hay(na)ku
during a workshop sponsored by the Philippine Scholars Program (PSP).
Founded by Gary W. King (Minnesota, USA), PSP began in 1994 with pri-
oritizing the education of children of political detainees and desapare-
cidos. It since has expanded to include the children from marginalized
groups encompassing farmers, urban poor, among others. Participants
in its workshops come from both high school and college-level students.
The workshop occurred during PSP's summer camp at the SVD retreat
house in Lapulapu City, Cebu, Philippines.

The hay(na)ku celebrated its 15th birthday in 2018, an event com-
memorated with readings, performances, exhibitions and a birthday
cake at the San Francisco and Saint Helena Public Libraries. Birthday
sponsors were Meritage Press, xPress(ed), Paloma Press (who published
my 2018 bilingual English-Spanish hay(na)ku book *One, Two, Three* with
translator Rebeka Lembo), Philippine American Writers & Artists, the
two libraries, and San Francisco Public Library's Filipino American Cen-
ter. For the year-long celebration, I am grateful for the hard work of cul-
tural activists Abraham Ignacio, Jr., Aileen Ibardaloza Cassinetto, Edwin
Lozada, Melinda Luisa de Jesus, Michelle Bautista, and Abigail Licad,
among others.

Nonetheless, I and some other poets who had engaged with the form in
its early years were surprised to begin 2018 and realize it to be the hay(na)
ku's 15th anniversary. "Many avant-garde creations don't last that long!"
observed Finnish poet-artist-musician Jukka-Pekka Kervinen, who has
published many contemporary poets and who resuscitated his publish-
ing house xPress(ed) to co-publish the form's anniversary anthology,

HAY(NA)KU 15 (2018). Some poets apparently never stopped writing in the form, and new poets kept coming to it! With 2018, the San Francisco Public Library's Filipino-American Center hosted an exhibition of hay(na)ku poems—an idea that later would be replicated at Saint Helena Public Library (my local library). Originally intended to be an anniversary show, the compilation of hay(na)ku posters featuring over 20 poets since has become a permanent exhibit at the San Francisco Public Library.

I am grateful to the 128 poets and translators whose works comprise *HAY(NA)KU 15*. The anthology presents poems in eight languages: English, Filipino, Finnish, Hindi, Polish, Portuguese, Romanian, and Spanish. The poets come from 13 countries: Australia, Canada, England, Finland, India, Luxembourg, Mexico, New Zealand, Philippines, Poland, Scotland, Thailand, and United States. I am also thankful to the 12 translators who, as part of the Poetry and Translation Seminar at the National Autonomous University of Mexico (UNAM), translated 36 poets from the now out-of-print *The First Hay(na)ku Anthology*. Their translations form the second section of the anthology as an all-Spanish collection of hay(na)ku.

As I've noted, the hay(na)ku takes the opposite of a colonizing approach when it does not force its single tercet form on others but is open to variations. Since 2003, poets from around the world have created such variations as

—"chained hay(na)ku" where the poem is comprised of more than one tercet

—"reverse hay(na)ku" where the word count for the tercet is 3, 2, 1 instead of 1, 2, 3. Charles Bernstein's term for this variation is "Ku(na) hay"

—"Flip-Flop Hay(na)ku," named by Vince Gotera, is a chained hay(na) ku where the stanzas flip-flop between 1 / 2 / 3 – word lines to 3 / 2 / 1- word lines

—"haybun" where the poem contains both tercet and prose

—"haibu(na)ku" by Thomas Fink, a haybun variation where the numbers align for six words for the hay(na)ku tercet and six sentences for the prose; or 12 words for the two tercets and 12 sentences for the prose; or 18 words for the three tercets and 18 sentences for the prose, and so on

—"ducktail hay(na)ku" where a tercet or sequence of tercets ends with a last stanza being a single line that can be as long as desired by the poet (the inspiration is a haircut where hair is trimmed short, except for a long strand dangling from the middle of the back of the head)

—"Hay(na)ku Sonnet" by Vince Gotera, a form created through four hay(na)ku tercets plus an ending couplet with three words per line. The closing couplet is a hay(na)ku where the one-word line and the two-word line have been concatenated in order to end up with 14 lines

—"Rippled Mirror" hay(na)ku where the first tercet with a 1, 2, 3 word count is followed by a tercet with a 3, 2, 1 word count and where the narrative content is somewhat reversed between the two tercets, for example, from my chapbook *To Be An Empire Is To Burn* (2017):

FERDINAND EDRALIN MARCOS
(Rippled Mirror Hay(na)ku #1)

"Power
corrupts absolutely"—
you provided proof.

Your life proved
"Absolute corruption
powers."

—"melting hay(na)ku" where the poem begins with the tercet form before the stanza(s) "melt" into prose poetry paragraphs, sentences or fragments

—"The Mayan Hay(na)ku" created by then 11-year-old Maya Fink whereby the first line has a word comprised of one letter, the second line two words each comprised of two letters, the third line three words each comprised of three letters, and so on for as long as the poet cares to take it

—"Sci(na)ku Tanka" (and reverse sci(na)ku tanka) was invented by Roxanne Barbour as a five-line poem with the word-per-line count of 1, 2, 3, 2, 1 (reverse would be 3, 2, 1, 2, 3).

—the internet's "moving hay(na)ku" proposed by Kari Kokko whereby, through the wonders of HTML, the lines move across the screen

—"abecedarian hay(na)ku" by Scott Glassman where each word begins with each succeeding letter in the English alphabet

—"worm hay(na)ku" by Ivy Alvarez, who describes it as "using letters that don't have tops" (b, d, f, h, i, j, k, l, t) or tails (g, j, p, q, y)

—Tagalog slang hay(na)ku by Marlon Unas Esguerra

—"Hay(na)koan" by Tom Beckett involving koans

—"cleave hay(na)ku" from Vince Gotera: two hay(na)ku side-by-side, where the hay(na)ku on the left is read as one poem, the hay(na)ku on the right is read as a second poem, and then both hay(na)ku are read as a third, combined poem—both first lines together, then the second lines, and finally both third lines

—"hay(na)ku with shadorma ending" created by Bastet of the blog *MindLoveMisery's Menagerie* (shadorma is a Spanish poetic form)

—"hay(na)ku sentence" proposed by Jean Vengua who notes, "A sentence based on hay(na)ku is brief; it would slip by with perhaps less of a sense of 'finish,' yet it has a certain impact. Here's one:

    Primaries are over; the crows alight.

—collaborations between poets and visual artists (which generated an anthology dedicated to such collaborations of three or more poets/artists, *The Chained Hay(na)ku* (2012))

—"sci(na)ku" which is hay(na)ku with a speculative element. A post to the Science Fiction Poetry Association's Facebook page on April 9, 2014,

credits Martin Tomlinson with the first ever published Sci(na)ku by the
Aphelion Webzine, April 2014

—"Spirals" by Chuck Brickley which is a poem formed by three hay(na)
ku tercets

—"systematic one-word hay(na)ku" by Uruguay-based poet Claude
Nguyen, like so:

> puños
> sound puños
> puños sound puño

—"Syllabic Hay(na)ku" inadvertently created by Amy Ray Pabalan who
counted syllables rather than words because she initially "misread the
description of Hay(na)ku"

—and visual or sculptural forms of the hay(na)ku, from visual poetry to
collages to paintings (e.g., Thomas Fink) to even a kitchen towel instal-
lation by Sandy and Barbara McIntosh.

As its history depicts, the hay(na)ku succeeded in becoming a com-
munity-based poetic form; this fits my own thoughts on the poem as a
space for engagement. Some favorite poetic projects are those where
I helped create a community. I feel this way because I think a poem
doesn't fully mature without a particular community called reader(s).
Poetry is (inherently) social.

Since becoming known outside the Flips listserve, most hay(na)ku
have been written by non-Filipinos. This is certainly a fine result, since
Poetry is not (or need not be) ethnic-specific and because I consider the
hay(na)ku to be a form made possible by my location in the diaspora.
I agree with Filipino poet-novelist Eric Gamalinda when he observes,
"The history of the Philippines is the history of the world."

Nonetheless, as word spreads, more Filipinos are taking on the hay(na)
ku. A professor at the University of the Philippines has contacted me
about the form and, as recently as 2023, I was informed that the hay(na)
ku was used at the College of San Mateo (California) for setting up its
Katipunan Learning Community that presents a culturally attuned cur-
riculum for Filipino-American students.

. . .

Haybun

My favorite variation, for personal reasons, has to be the haybun, a com-
bination of hay(na)ku tercet and prose (in the same way the phoneti-
cally similar "haibun" combines a haiku and prose). My husband and
I were blessed to adopt our son, Michael, when he was 13 years old.
From Colombia where he'd lived in an orphanage, he spoke only Span-
ish so that he had to learn English during his first years with us. In 8th
grade, he was encouraged to expand his English vocabulary by learning
25 new words a week. After he finished this project, I asked to see his
list of newly acquired words. From his list of about 900 words (and with
his permission), I created hay(na)ku tercets. I then wrote a paragraph as
inspired by the randomly chosen words and their random combinations.
The resulting haybuns became the first haybun collection, my book *147
Million Orphans* (2014). The book's title refers to how, though no one
really knows the number of orphans worldwide, a common estimate at
the time was 147 million. Here is a sample haybun that explores and/or
responds to some of the issues I discovered while researching interna-
tional adoption; not all references relate to our family's experience, but
instead to the humanitarian disaster of there being too many orphans in
the world as well as the psychic wounds from orphanhood:

> *television*
> *screening insightful*
> *prescient melancholy evasive*

> If you were a sleeping bird in Madagascar, a certain species
> of moth might drink your tears through a fearsome proboscis
> shaped like a harpoon. They'd insert their tools beneath your
> eyelids. They would drink *avidly*. You were a rapt presence
> as you met this species through the grainy television screen
> used to babysit hundreds of orphans. After the television
> darkened, no genius would be required to explain your
> prescient conclusion: you will attempt to evade too much
> in this life, you will fail, *there is no other life.* ~~You, sadly, will
> come to prefer silk, even polyester, doppelgangers to roses
> that otherwise would shrivel.~~ Your insights will always arise

from the sheen of rain-drenched pavements. For example,
that one can weep without the aid of nightmares—that one
can weep in the safest haven, or even the small heavens that
still and do manage to pock-mark our mortal planet.

Eight years later, another haybun collection would be released—a book in Macedonian by Dijana Petkova whose book's translated-into-English title is *Dragon Tamer* (2022). Dijana's book was released in Skopje with a related theater performance. I am moved that poets are not only writing hay(na)ku but writing *books* of hay(na)ku poems. To the best of my knowledge, as of 2023, if one includes miniature books, there have been 25 hay(na)ku-dedicated books released by 19 poets in six countries.

. . .

Writing Tip

Six words in three lines. Minimalist but not simple. For offering a tip for writing good hay(na)ku, I suggest poets avoid making an article—like "the," "a," or "an"—comprise a single line. Each line should still be interesting. To quote José Garcia Villa, the most talented Filipino poet writing in English during the 20th century or first century in which English was widely used by Filipinos, "Each word should be necessary." The hay(na)ku sheds a spotlight on each line to make clear: each line should feel poetically *urgent*. An article by itself is generally too passive to create a striking line.

. . .

Hay(na)ku as an Introduction to Poetry

While the hay(na)ku has been taught at universities and high schools by me and others, its deceptively simple form also makes it a good children's introduction to poetry. The form can be introduced through a simple worksheet that was brought to my attention by two parents, both poets, who decided to teach hay(na)ku to the classes of their young children. Their worksheet features blank lines upon which the kids can scrawl words:

HAY(NA)KU POETRY

—————————

————————— —————————

————————— ————————— —————————

The poet-parents describe their experiences as follows:

MICHELLE BAUTISTA:
I did a workshop for kindergarteners at an Oakland Public School. We used the worksheet. In addition, I brought a bag of objects. Kids would pull out objects and hold and study them for a minute. Then they would write any six words to describe the object. We wrote one word each on a sticky note. Then the kids could put the sticky notes on the spaces on the worksheet and move them around until they liked the result.

MELINDA LUISA DE JESUS:
I did my first hay(na)ku workshop at Walden School in Berkeley for [daughter] Malaya's 3rd grade class in 2018. I introduced the form with examples including a hay(na)ku about hay(na)ku:

Only
six words—
and it's done

I then drew the worksheet on a large easel pad for class-generated hay(na)kus. Then the kids brainstormed their own poems individually, which they shared. Poems about pets and siblings were very popular with this group!

I've also used this worksheet for hay(na)ku workshops at
Oakland School for the Arts in 2021 (high school students and
staff), and at the Berkeley Women of Color conference in 2022.

I was pleased to learn of Michelle and Melinda's experiences as they
attest to the hay(na)ku's inviting nature. When poetry becomes an invi-
tation, poetry also behaves in a manner that's the opposite of colonial-
ism's divisive nature. Through poetry's invitation, communities can
form.

Chapter 3

MURDER DEATH RESURRECTION

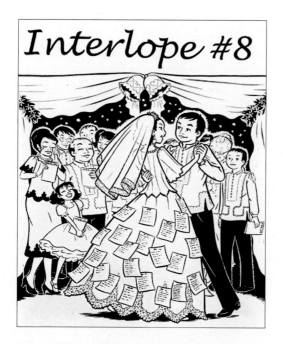

My husband Tom grimaced as he turned his eyes away. I, on the other hand, bent in laughter, tears leaking down my cheeks. We had just seen an extremely hairy man itching in my 15-year-old wedding dress of white satin festooned with seed pearls, sequins, and lace. In August 2002, we were in LOCUS, a performing arts space in San Francisco, where South Asian poet Amar Ravva had stripped down to his boxer shorts before gingerly putting on my wedding gown with its ornate bodice and voluminous skirt.

"I had wonderful memories of watching you walk down the aisle towards me as we got married," Tom said. "Your damn poetry just ruined those memories. How can I unsee this!?"

Amar had volunteered to wear my dress as part of a "happening" that featured my latest poem-sculpture: the interactive "Poem Tree" that symbolized my commitment to poetry through a symbolic marriage to "Mr/s Poetry." "Poem Tree" was modeled after a rite in Filipino and Latino weddings wherein guests pin money on the bride's and groom's outfits. The ritual relates to guests offering financial aid to a couple beginning a new life together. For "Poem Tree," printouts of poems were pinned onto the dress to symbolize how poetry, too, feeds the world. In prior happenings, those wearing my dress were Filipina female poets to reflect my status—Natalie Concepcion (at an event at Sonoma State University) and Barbara Jane Reyes (at an event at Pusod Gallery, Berkeley). For the third happening sponsored by the Alliance of Emerging Creative Artists and *Interlope: A Journal of Asian America Poetics and Issues* edited by Summi Kaipa, Amar was chosen because poetry need not be ethnic- or gender-specific.

Nonetheless, Amar, while petite enough to fit into my dress, was quite hirsute. His physicality offered a (wonderfully) dissonant contrast against my wedding gown that was created by a Mexican dressmaker in Los Angeles. That dressmaker, found by my mother, created elaborate dresses for *quinceañeras*, 15th birthday celebrations for girls that's widely celebrated in Latin America and other Hispanic communities. Mom went overboard as she helped choose the dress' baroque style—this was her one shot to be Mother of the Bride since I was our family's only daughter. If my dress was cheese, it was of the oozing, triple crème variety. Its detailed, multilayered style only highlighted the oddness of the dress draping the shoulders of a bearded man with a bemused expression and flat, black shoes that peeked out beneath the skirt. Several times during the happening, I had to force myself not to look at Amar since the sight of his black chest hair poking out from my dress' pearl-strewn décolletage usually sent me roaring in amusement. Whew! Was I glad Mom was not in town to witness Amar in my dress!

To reflect my belief that a poem transcends its author's autobiography, "Poem Tree" used my dress to reflect my "I," but different poets wore it. Further expanding on how a poem's persona is more than its author's, the poems used during the happenings were written by other poets. During 2001-2002, I managed an open call for poems. Over 100 poets representing 13 countries and about half of the U.S. states responded. I printed their poems and, from the printouts, cut out sections in the shape of a Filipino peso to reflect the cultural origin of the ritual. During the happenings, audience members pinned my dress with the peso-sized segments that featured the titles and authors of each poem. The rest of the printed pages presented the poems and were taken by guests as wedding souvenirs.

I also wrote to friends (and, through this book, make this same suggestion to you readers): "One pins poems, not just money, on a newlywed couple's wedding outfits because Poetry, too, is a source of sustenance. If some of your friends get married and their festivities include this rite, you might bring poems to pin on their outfits! Poetry is not just to be read and written but also to be lived!"

I was delighted to learn that some couples, indeed, included a "Poem Tree" aspect to their wedding festivities. This result, along with others having shared that "Poem Tree" caused them to look at poetry in a new way, or even pay attention to poetry for the first time, reflects my desire to expand poetry's involvement in people's lives.

. . .

Randomness and the allowance of elements not under one's control are integral to my poetry practice. Audience response, for example, is not something a poet or any artist can control. Such facets are meaningful to me as decolonized practices, symbols of the opposite of colonialism's controlling nature. This aspect also can be seen in how I title poems, such as for my poem, "*Nerium Oleander*, Shorter Than Kerima."

In our garden, the oleander shrub is massive, about 18 feet high and 24 feet wide. I usually ignore its greenery as backdrop for much of the year, but in the summer, it grabs any backyard visitor's attention since it sprouts, as I wrote in the poem about it,

> braggadocious clusters of blooms
> radiating whites, pinks and reds
> easily holding up the non-fallen sky

Four stanzas later, however, the poem switched gears to refer to a murder in the Philippines:

> Stunned, I learned even the smallest fragment
> from your thin petals can send my dogs
> to join you, Kerima Lorena Tariman

killed by the Armed Forces' 70th Infantry
Battalion in Silay City, Negros Occidental
on August 20, 2021—the evening before

the 38th anniversary of the assassination
of Benigno Aquino, Jr., sparking other People's
Revolutions around the world . . .

I did not expect that my poem inspired by the magnificently sprout-
ing *Nerium Oleander* would lead to the murder of the 42-year-old activ-
ist and poet who was wounded in a battle between the New People's
Army and the Philippine military in Negros Occidental, Philippines. The
former managing editor of the University of the Philippines' *Philippine
Collegian*, Kerima and her husband, poet-musician Ericson Acosta (who
was killed about three months later in similar circumstances), lived in
Negros where they fought for the poor and landless. Negros has long
suffered from a sugar hacienda lifestyle as well as polluted mining; the
province once received global attention for a 78% infant malnourish-
ment rate during the 1970s/80s. In fact, as an undergraduate student
at Barnard College, I wrote a political science paper on the conflict of
interests between politicians charged with guiding the country's devel-
opment on behalf of the entire population while belonging to wealthy
families whose status quo they were incentivized to preserve if not
enhance. Perhaps not surprisingly but nonetheless irresponsibly, since
my college years the gap between rich and poor has widened. My poem
ends with the hope:

Kerima's flower shall be generous with seeds
blossoming to grow a Homeland no longer
Imaginary, no longer abstracted by corruption

We are a people as hardy as you and, soon
our Motherland shall be watered by other
sources than the veins of sacrificed poets.

I am glad my poem remembers Kerima Lorena Tariman. Though I did
not plan or anticipate the result, I can understand how a mention of kill-
ing or its possibility—for example, by the oleander's poisonous petals—
and as enhanced by my decades-long awareness of Negros' plight might

evoke the revolutionary working and dying in the province known as "Sugarbowl of the Philippines."

Nor am I surprised my would-be flower poem traveled elsewhere and far—it's what can happen when the poet doesn't try to control the poem. In considering this effect, I recalled a book by Maureen Owen, *Zombie Notes* (1985), where titles don't always remain atop poems. In another book, *The No-Travels Journal* (1975), the title of her poem, "Paris Blues," is placed at the bottom of the verse. That format exemplifies how my better poems work: I don't know their titles until I've completed writing them (or their first drafts). When I began writing my poem, I certainly did not anticipate that it would end up being titled "*Nerium Oleander, Shorter Than Kerima.*"

The poems themselves will provide their titles. It seems so basic to me now, but not if one understands that I'm like many who've been introduced to poems as something that's *about* something. But to approach a poem's creation that way is, for me, too paradigmatic or stifling. The poem often transcends authorial intent and must be free to go where it chooses.

I've learned that my role as a poet is to capture a burst of something— whether it's a feeling or a resonant single word or an image (like the gloriously flowering oleander)—that would open the door to the rest of the poem. My poems *become* due to their writing process, e.g., a word surfaces only because of the prior word or phrases. There's a saying, "Poems write themselves," and such has been my experience.

As a result, much of my job as a poet takes place before I begin the poem. My job is to educate myself on as many topics as possible, engage in a wide variety of experiences, hone my skills at observation, and meditate over the significance of a variety of events—not for writing a poem but for being better in the world through a basking in experience. All this knowledge and experience are filed in my brain as raw material for when I finally write the poem, e.g., the information on Negros Occidental which had marinated in my mind for three decades. In the actual creation of the poem, I trust in having filed enough mental material for the poem to access as it chooses.

Obviously, the more content there is in that mental file, the better the poem is served. As a poet, I believe in education for education's sake for avoiding cliches and sourcing new metaphors. As an example, for no reason besides education, I learned about black holes, specifically, that if one is able to witness its gravity, one would see objects falling into those holes in falls that seem never to end. The idea of a *permanent falling* resonated and came to be included in several of my poems.

  After the poem informs me of its last word, I then discover its title. But I first had to begin the poem with an openness that would not prejudge how the poem might conclude itself. This relates to my faith in an inclusive poetry practice because, as I wrote within my poem "Faith" whose body included three underlined blank spaces for the reader to write on,

  To bring the poem into the world
  Is to bring the world into the poem

                         . . .

Murder Death Resurrection (MDR)

As a poet, being open to the world, including its random or unanticipated elements, facilitates my continuous search for ways to make poems in different ways or ways not limited by tradition. Again, I wasn't invested in abiding by inherited English or English structures in making new poems. Still, while interested in creating spaces through which others create poems—whether it's the hay(na)ku or projects like "Poem Tree" that generate the call for others' poems—I naturally have been writing my own poems. I believe that for poetry (and many other disciplines), one needs to be a practitioner to be a theorist, and I've been prolific with both the number of poems written and poetry books released.

  But in 2013, I was weary of everything I'd created. So, I decided to "murder" my poems—specifically, 27 poetry collections published up to that point—in an attempt to find yet another way for creating poems. For this attempt, I wanted to deepen my interrogation of English for facilitating 20th century U.S. colonialism in the Philippines. I also wanted to develop a consciously closer link to the Filipino indigenous value of "Kapwa." "Kapwa" refers to "shared self" or "shared identity" whereby everyone and everything is connected[1]. Thus, Kapwa is relevant to the idea underpinning the hay(na)ku and other poetry projects that enable the reader to be the author.

  Creation can first mean destruction. But I wasn't looking for gore. I conceived of murder to be *forgetting*—to murder my old poems by forgetting them so that I could create new ones not shackled by what I'd previously written.

How to deliberately forget? Well, to forget my poems, I read through every one of my poetry books and chapbooks and, as I read, I kept writing that I forgot them. The result is a group of 1,167 lines with nearly all beginning with the words "I forgot." Following this phrase was whatever surfaced during my reading—from excerpts to my real time reactions to what I was reading. The lines form a database that opens with what surfaced from reading my first poetry chapbook, *After the Egyptians Determined the Shape of the World is a Circle* (1996)[2]:

I forgot I became a connoisseur of alleys.

I forgot I knew the back alleys of this neighborhood,
where beggars made their beds, whose cats
stole their food, which doorways provided for or
grabbed the fragile into a hold of cruelty.

I forgot why lovers destroy children to parse
the philosophy of separation.

I forgot the glint from the fang of a wild boar as he lurked behind
shadows in a land where it only takes one domino to fall.

I forgot how quickly civilization can disappear—as
swiftly as the shoreline from an oil spill birthed from a
twist of the wrist by a drunk vomiting over the helm.

I use the word "database" because the group is a source of new poems, whether by me or others. When the database is unused, the lines are dead. But if the lines are used for new poems—lifted out of the database—they become resurrected. They are resurrected into new poems. Thus, I titled my project "Murder Death Resurrection" (MDR).

MDR's conceit is that any combination of the lines is a legitimate poem—from the shortest possible combination of a couplet to a 1,167-line poem. Whether or not MDR merits its conceit, the project generated six published books and four chapbooks in its first five years[3]. The first, *44 RESURRECTIONS* (2014), includes couplets, while *AMNESIA: Somebody's Memoir* (2016) is a book-length poem utilizing all the lines (*AMNESIA* orders the lines to abide by sections that are formatted to evoke chapters). MDR's official monograph can be considered to be *MURDER DEATH RESURRECTION* (2018), which features the database of all 1,167 lines in the order they first were written, as well as other prose about the project such as a Study Guide.

For its ability to effect poems, I also refer to MDR as MDR Poetry Generator. I would write, rather, *make* poems by blindly pointing to lines from a printout of the database. Through this random way of creating combinations from some of the 1,167 lines, I published individual poems as well as released collections from nine different publishers. Other poems generated visual poetry versions, some of which inaugurated *h&*, a journal of visual/concrete poetry; others showed up in an exhibition of visual poetry and arts, "Chromatext Rebooted" at the Cultural Center of the Philippines (Manila, 2016-2017).[4]

Since 2013, when I began MDR, results have exceeded expectations. Because of the random way the poems were created and despite various publications, I kept waiting for combinations to fail in such a way as to have the MDR poem be judged as sheer nonsense. But such failure didn't seem to be a significant factor. Indeed, certain combinations which do not move me as a reader found receptive readers. For instance, I do not find this two-line combination (the first line incorporates a list of names) to be particularly effective:

> I forgot my father is not and never has been
> President of the United States:
>> Harry S. Truman
>> Dwight D. Eisenhower
>> John F. Kennedy
>> Lyndon B. Johnson
>> Richard M. Nixon
>> Gerald Ford
>> Jimmy Carter
>> Ronald Reagan
>> George Bush
>> Bill Clinton
>> George W. Bush
>> Barack Obama
>
> I forgot music became a jail.

Yet at least two readers admired the couplet and said so in public. Reviewer Alan Baker called it "powerful"[5] and interviewer Thomas Fink stated, "I appreciate the juxtaposition because the 'music' of the names leads to an aspect of what they signify, metonymies attached to them; Presidents are 'jailed' in their often ridiculously difficult historical circumstances, and people in the U.S. and the world can be 'imprisoned' by decisions that these leaders make."[6] I remain unenthused over the couplet, but certainly won't censor Alan and Tom from responding as they wish to (my) poems.

No doubt, part of MDR's success was the scaffolding provided by the phrase "I forgot"—the phrase's repetition ends up facilitating a poetic rhythm to what are de facto list poems. The use of "I forgot" was a tactic inspired by Tom Beckett's poem, "I Forgot," in his book ~~Dipstick~~ *(Diptych)* (2014)[7].

MDR also reflects my long-standing interests in abstract and cubist language as a way to interrogate English for having been a colonizing tool. Through my perceptions of abstraction and cubism, I've written poems whose lines are not fixed in order and, indeed, can be reordered. When I first began as a poet, I was very interested in the prose poem form and in writing paragraphs that can be reordered within the poem. For example, from my first U.S.-published book of prose poetry, *Reproductions of the Empty Flagpole* (2002)[8] is this poem:

GREY, SURREPTITIOUSLY

Sometimes I am not tired. And I begin to pace the perimeter of Manhattan. I am always drawn to the East River, how the water is consistently grey and this sensibility mists over the entire East Side: it swathes the total territory in a wool suit. And it makes me recall interchangeable cities in Eastern Europe where the only spots of color are offered by tiny pastries silently waiting behind glass. Afterwards, I finish with memories of museum exhibits salvaging dusty armors from the crusades of a different century.

I *am* surprised that I linger in this part of the city, that the river's surface loses its drabness to enfold me like cashmere. Unexpectedly, patchouli and cinnabar begin to linger in the air though I see no one dodging my careful

steps. I feel the birth of pearls in tropical ocean beds
tended by boys burnt by the sun. Then I feel one pearl's
inexplicable caress in the hollow between my breasts.

A woman rounds a bend and sees me. I pause by a white
birch tree stripped by winter of its leaves. She smiles as she
approaches. I wish to feel my fingers loosening her jeweled
combs. Already, I can feel her hair curl shyly against my
fingers like the breaking of surreptitious surf. No words
would be spoken, but a window from an anonymous
building would open to loosen the faint tinkling of piano
notes. They would be plucked from the highest scale.

My fingers would turn blue in the cold. They would freeze in
their fraught pose, laid against a stranger's scented cheek while
her hair would continue to flutter in a faint breeze. And her
lashes would trap a beginning snow. And her life-generating
breaths would occur through parted lips. And her eyes, too,
would be the deadening of a river: translucent and grey

I believe "Grey, Surreptitiously" would be equally effective (albeit with different resonance) if the paragraphs were in a different order, say, if paragraphs 1, 2, 3, and 4 were ordered as 2, 4, 1, and 3.

Such fluidity of language was/is, for me, the metaphorical opposite of language used for colonizing—language used by colonial masters to *order* those they'd subjugated. Such orders usually have specific intentions as regards enforcing behavior and policies, among others. MDR's way of creating poems shifts emphasis away from author to reader in determining the poem's effectiveness—metaphorically the opposite of colonizing as the position of the speaker/author is destabilized.

MDR also affirms what I call "Kapwa Poetics"—a poetics based on the indigenous Filipino value, Kapwa, of interconnection among all beings and things. There's an image from pre-colonial Philippine times of a human standing with a hand lifted upwards; if you happened to be at a certain distance from the human and took a snapshot, it would look like the human was touching the sky. Filipino novelist N.V.M. Gonzalez mythologizes this human as a creature who, by being rooted onto the planet but also touching the sky, is connected to everything in the universe and across all time, including that the human is rooted to the past and future—indeed, there is no unfolding of time.(9) In that moment, all of existence—past, present and future—has coalesced into a singular moment, a single gem with an infinite expanse. This is the space in which I strive to write poems, thus my calling Kapwa (partly) a "poetics." In my poetry, I strive in part to explore/reveal the interconnection of all beings and things—through poetry, I wish for no one or nothing to be alien to me.

I extrapolate "Kapwa Poetics" from N.V.M. Gonzalez's notion of the Filipino as a "mythic man." Scholar Katrin de Guia summarizes this important contribution by one of the Philippines' National Artists in literature as a "mythic person" who is "content with 'Being-at-Home-in-the-World and Being-Human.' . . . Gonzalez points out that Filipinos are a people whose past is rooted in the cyclical time of their ancient myths. During this era of wandering seas and strange storms, life went on in cycles of planting and reaping, sailing and arriving, walking and finding. These were . . . times of primordial oneness with the world, where the sky was so near that people could touch it with their hands. The ancient ones were able to connect to anyone and everything at all times."(9)

Linear time was introduced to the Philippines with the encroachment of Spanish colonizers who enforced Catholic belief. But while Christianity's time-bound basis caused a dilution of the ancient mythic self, memory remains. Thus, Filipinos favor two levels of time: the sacred and the profane. "Sacred time," according to Gonzalez, "is a point of freedom and abundance—the suspended moment in a time of utmost creativity . . . where man and creation are one." That is, says de Guia,

> From the wholistic perspective of the mythic man, the world was just created. No divisions separate the past from the now, the adults from the children, the men from their myths and their dreams, men from their fellow men of the men from their fellow beings. There is no need for walls to separate the creator and the created. Microcosm and macrocosm are but one—a continuity. Some people call this ancestral Filipino outlook Kapwa (the shared Self).[9]

For practicing Kapwa Poetics, I've tried to write poems within the space of "sacred time," such as a poem entitled "Sacred Time" in 2010, where the persona moves effortlessly from the closed space of a kitchen to the openness of "days of / touching sunlit / sky."[10] Relatedly, Kapwa Poetics encourages that there is no dispute between intentionalized authorship and the randomness with which the lines are combined from The MDR Poetry Generator—for, *All is One and One is All.*

Finally, if indigenous time is not split between past, present, and future, how then can one forget? That element is reflected in the MDR poems which begin with "I forgot _____." Once one articulates what one is supposedly forgetting, isn't one then remembering?

· · ·

To date, and to my surprise, I've received only positive responses to the MDR project, such as the reviews for *MURDER DEATH RESUR-RECTION*. But I was conscious that most readers of the MDR poems are those in the so-called "poetry world" which, at a minimum, means poets or poetry-readers who are used to the idiosyncrasies that abound in poetry. Thus, I began introducing MDR to non-"literary" audiences through workshops and class visits. In March 2018, I visited two high school math classes to introduce poetry while offering MDR as an example of the mathematical concept of permutations (or possible combinations, in this case, of poetic lines from MDR's database). In April 2018, I also brought MDR to a local bookstore for a reading/workshop, as well as to a college humanities course on "Home and Belonging in the 21st Century." I preferred audiences beyond literary-oriented groups to reflect Kapwa's notion of interconnection.

During my MDR events, I presented each student or participant with *MURDER DEATH RESURRECTION* where each line in the database is presented in a numbered fashion. I asked them to formulate poems by picking a group of numbers at random between "1" and "1,167." They then found the lines in the book associated with each number and wrote down the lines. After determining each poem's text, participants then collaborated on titling the poems (I thought the titling of a poem would help show whether the participant found something meaningful in the result). What was intriguing to me was that not once did someone challenge any of the resulting poems to be a "failed poem," even as we were using a radically different method to making poems than through conventional ways based on authorial decisions.[11]

The live exercises mirrored the book's "Introduction," where I suggest to readers that they pick any combination of numbers with the lowest being 1, and the highest being 1,167. In the book, I made an example of picking 1, 12, 735, 51. The lines associated with the numbers are

1: I forgot I became a connoisseur of alleys.

12: I forgot the years when I wore uniforms of darkened wool shaped by machines, lined by grey.

735: I forgot how stars became asterisks to matters best left in the dark. I forgot the tirelessness of shame.

51: I forgot fingertips deliquesced to black velvet from constantly rolling tobacco leaves—the only luxury many farmers could afford.

I excised the numbers for the resulting new poem. I also indicated about this example:

I often create the poems' titles after the poems are made, which would seem to be the logical strategy for titles versus a title created because the poet wants to write verse that manifests that title's theme. Through The MDR Poetry Generator, the poet does not know what the poem will look like until the poem is created. So, for the above example, I can title it, say, "How Darkness Grows (Version 25)" to create this poem:

HOW DARKNESS GROWS (VERSION 25)

I forgot I became a connoisseur of alleys.

I forgot the years when I wore uniforms of darkened wool shaped by machines, lined by grey.

I forgot how stars became asterisks to matters best left in the dark. I forgot the tirelessness of shame.

I forgot fingertips deliquesced to black velvet
from constantly rolling tobacco leaves—the
only luxury many farmers could afford.

I thought of the title by noting the shades of (metaphorical)
darkness that seem to get darker as the poem unfolds—that
is, from the dimness of alleys to the depressing sameness of
an office worker's (the "suit") life to shame to the hardship
experienced by poor farmers. There are, of course, many
more types of darkness than what are noted in the poem,
hence my parenthetical "(Version 25)." Also, I thought that
by hinting at the many versions of darkness that exist, the
parenthetical phrase actually embodies more darkness.

Along with the book's Introduction, I incorporated an "Educator's
Guide" with "Suggested Study Questions & Workshop" because I also
hoped MURDER DEATH RESURRECTION would be used by others to
conduct workshops or class exercises.

. . .

The following presents Field Reports from introducing MDR to the
public:

MATH CLASSES AT BERKELEY HIGH SCHOOL
March 2018

I visited two sessions of International Baccalaureate (IB) Math SL2, a
combined calculus/statistics class. I enthusiastically approached high
school students since I wanted open minds as regards what defines a
poem and thought, rightly or wrongly, that such open minds might be
facilitated by youth and/or inexperience. I was interested in, as much as
possible, a direct engagement between the reader and the MDR poem
without the mediation of whatever preconceptions they may have
(including, been taught) about poetry.

The Berkeley High classes were taught by Carol Dorf, a poet-math
teacher. Most of the students were 12th graders, with a few 11th graders.
We divided each class of about 30 kids into groups of about four. Within
their groups, each student picked two numbers at random between 1

and 1,167. Each group then lined up their numbers and wrote the lines associated with the numbers in the book. Each group then was asked to read, discuss and come up with a title for the resulting poem. Titling the poem was a way for the students to discuss what the group of lines may signify to them.

I didn't say what defines a poem. I just "instructed" as a given that the group of lines they'd create would make up a legitimate poem. Each group then appointed a member who would read the poem to the class. Another member then presented a summary of how the group members reacted to the "poem" they'd just made.

Everyone, or their speaking representatives, responded thoughtfully. Nor did anyone succumb to the reductive binary as regards the poem to judge the result as good versus bad. In fact, they all reacted matter-of-factly to MDR as a legitimate way to create a poem. I hope that the activity planted a seed in the young students that poetry need not be alien to their future lives.

Here's one example of poems created at Berkeley High:

A MASK

I forgot men holding babies upside down by their legs to
smash them across the same trees that received their piss.

I forgot desiring journeys to far off places to discover
what is missing in the commonplace around me.

I forgot a limp laundry line almost invisible in the grey.

I forgot the 18-year-old Diego Rivera eating a woman for
the first time—through cannibalism, not cunnilingus.

Oh paradox! Such a reliable door to the unknown.

I forgot I became a connoisseur of alleys.

I forgot why lovers destroy children to parse
the philosophy of separation.

I forgot how quickly civilization can disappear, as swiftly

as the shoreline from an oil spill birthed from a twist
of the wrist by a drunk vomiting over the helm.

. . .

SONOMA STATE UNIVERSITY (SSU)
April 2018

At SSU, I visited "Home and Belonging in the 21st Century," a freshman
humanities course taught by Leny Strobel. She described it as where
"our main focus is decolonization via ethnoautobiography. The stu-
dents worked on the themes of ancestral roots, historical shadow mate-
rial, dreams, spirituality, place, nature, community, mythic stories, sex
and gender issues. Our latest discussions focus on post-oppositionality
(beyond binary thinking/ Ana Louise Keating), mestizaje, nepantlera,
hybrid identities (Gloria Anzaldúa), feminist materialism+quantum the-
ory+indigenous wisdom (Bayo Akomolafe). We are trying to encourage
creativity and imagination when it comes to thinking about social justice
issues (race, class, etc) so that we may move away from 'us vs. them'."

At SSU, I presented on both MDR and the "hay(na)ku." The two forms
share in common an openness to difference through, respectively, Kapwa
and the reader's ability to vary the basic hay(na)ku tercet.

The nearly 60 students were divided into groups, and each group
was asked to create poems through the MDR, in the same manner as
described for Berkeley High. As well, we engaged in a hay(na)ku-writ-
ing exercise. My first take-away from my experience at SSU was how so
many students were living with so much stress. The many types of pres-
sure included "Deep Grief," a phrase for how one personalizes how the
environment is damaged—as affirmed by one student who, after class,
showed me her journal where she grieved over the effects of climate
change. More heartening were the levels of interest and fascination that
surprised me—and, in some cases, I suspect surprised the students, too.

Here is a sample hay(na)ku from my class visit:

HAY(NA)KU

Ignorance
stems from
an unwatered seed

Leny Strobel also provided the students with an "extra credit" oppor-
tunity by writing a paper engaging with MDR. Each paper would include
a poem written through MDR as well as the student's analysis of the
poem. This sampling of responses clearly reveals how the students—
perhaps for the first time—responded with openness to a poem:

> "reading this poem shows to me that we have let
> the colonizers win because they have made us
> forget about our culture, identity and home"

> "The third [line] means that there is a battle to
> becoming something, the last meant that not
> everything turns out the way it seems"

> "When I reread the poem, I can sense a heartbreak or also a
> feeling of lowliness. This emerges memories with my mother . . ."

From the above responses, students learned how poetry can surface
thoughts from their unconscious as well as to use it as a springboard
into unanticipated meditations over a variety of topics. Hopefully, this
role of poetry will prolong their interest in poetry, itself a positive and
even healing factor insofar as poetry offers one way to address difficult
and complicated matters.

. . .

EAST WIND BOOKS READING & WORKSHOP
May 2018

East Wind Books (EWB) offered another chance to live-test MDR—and
this was the first time where most of the audience were poets or those
with more interests in poetry than the students I visited in Berkeley
High and SSU. At EWB, I divided the audience into three groups. I then
gave each group the same instructions of picking numbers at random
between 1 and 1,167, finding the lines with those numbers and organiz-
ing them into poems. As always, after putting the poems together, they
were asked to title them.

After each group created a poem, a representative read the poem to
the crowd. After each reading, I asked the other two groups the question,

"Was that a legitimate poem?" In all cases, everyone said that what was created indeed was/is a poem. Several also expressed surprise at MDR's effectiveness, to which I admitted my relief that all of the poems were deemed legitimate poems. I noted, "This is an experiment I keep waiting to fail."

San Francisco Poet Laureate Kim Shuck, another reader at the event, jokingly replied, "Don't worry. Sooner or later, it will fail."

MDR's failure is a potential that hangs over the project. But I feel MDR *also* should fail. For some poems do fail, or some poems succeed for some readers and fail for other readers. Yet, I'm still waiting to witness MDR's failure! That Kapwa is strong! The interconnection of all things and creatures is simply undisputable.

. . .

What can poetry do? Many things, and certainly among them is how poetry can make you think about matters that only a particular poem can surface for you. Poetry, in other words, can open you up to new modes of thinking/feeling/viewing/ . . . and hopefully then a newly better way of living. Perhaps those who've written MDR poems would consider the implications of how a poem effectively surfaces from random choices, including our hidden but real connections with each other, including strangers. Perhaps that realization can help move them to strengthen their connections with others, and subsequently form new communities or take better care of their environments.

This element about poetry—*effecting positive change*—is perhaps the element to which scholars and critics pay the least attention since it's not based on the words that make up a poem. It's not based on the visible, e.g., text. Its effect relies significantly on the reader's subjectivity, which cannot be gauged by looking at the poem itself. This is why I liken the poem to a snapshot and poetry to a movie. Poetry as movie unfolds based on how the reader(s) engages (or not) with a poem. And it's tough for third-party analysts to discuss this "movie" since one cannot foretell the entirety of a movie based on a single snapshot or screenshot from it.

MDR doesn't just talk, but walks this notion of poetry as well as the notion of interconnectedness. No connection can be made based merely on my singular "I" as the author. Connections can be made only if space exists and is used for the reader's response, opinions, and feelings. MDR tested these theoretical concerns and did not—yet—find humanity wanting in its ability to be open to new and random elements. There surely is a lesson or lessons here in how one might navigate through this often cold world. That lesson, in Strobel's words, would be to avoid the "us vs. them" point of view.

· · ·

As it turns out, other readers would come to write poems through the MDR, though not necessarily in combinatorial ways—this result, too, is fine with me as poetry should be flexible. Berkeley High math instructor Carol Dorf ended up writing poems by using lines from MDR's database as starting points to new poems. Here's one:

I FORGOT THE TURNKEY TO THE VOID

I forgot the word "permutation"
and the way it leads to
an endless dinner party

You said speed measures
how fast something is travelling
I asked, "where are you going?"

You never did drive like a person
who understands momentum.

A party consists of at least two.
Who's the guest? Who's the host?

I appreciate the ending to Carol's poem for questioning a binary. It can be true that someone who began as a guest may end up being the host if, say, that person begins to ensure that others are having a good time by introducing people or with wise interventions into various discussions. The poem's last line—its example—shows a refusal to accept binaries as they are, in the way that MDR also proposes fluidity over binaries.

Leny Strobel took the same approach as Carol for creating new poems—she wrote a 100-page journal with all the entries rippling forth from an MDR line chosen at random. Leny's journal was later published as *GLIMPSES: A Poetic Memoir* (2019). Here's one example:

3.19.18

692   *I forgot him singing a shivering woman*
with no defense as soldiers arrive to do what they
did to her and her too-young daughters.

There stood a silent witness to the horrors done to women.

I've just returned from a weekend retreat with
indigenous women elders and young indigenous women
that was quickly summoned in the light of a #metoo
moment within the local native community.

In the circle, one after another, twenty-five women said:
     I was molested
     I was raped
     I was abused
     I was betrayed

     By men in the community.
     Men who are leaders
     Men who are protected by other women
     Men who are damaged

Tears flowed.

In the end, soothed by the words of a wise elder.

     The perpetrators have done things to your body.
     But they took nothing from you.
     They didn't take the stardust in you.
     Remember your strength and your Source.
     Cry. Let the tears flow.
     That is how we become human.

     But you are warriors.
     You will rise up.
     You will end this scourge in your life.
     We will heal our communities.

Other respected poets came to write new poems through the MDR, including Anne Gorrick, Jim Leftwich, Mike Gullickson, and Audrey Ward. Joey Madia, in reviewing MDR, even crafted a poem following instructions in the book's Introduction. Another poet, Erica Goss, was inspired to create her own poetry database.

Despite all this proof of MDR's effectiveness, I'll always have a space for doubt in my mind until all possible combinations—and poems—have been generated through MDR and judged by readers. To date, I've created about 140 poems through MDR. The total number of poems (in math jargon, "permutations") possible to be created through the MDR database can only be estimated since it is a huge sum. According to approximation formulas applied to MDR by Carl Ericson (my son's former high school math tutor) and Errol Koenig (then a student at Johns Hopkins Applied Mathematics & Statistics Department), MDR's possible total number of poems is a number that has 3,011 digits. Errol, for one, derived the number through the equation 1146!-1146, a number that roughly rounds to 1.129300103 E+3010 (that is, 1.129300103 times 10 to the 3,010th power)!

Scale has always been one of my concerns, specifically radical expanse and duration, for I believe that prolonged periods of attention will surface elements in a project that are possible only because of duration. I love knowing of the huge sum of poems that could be generated by MDR because its "poetry generator" facet was partly inspired by Nick Montfort's and Stephanie Strickland's poetry generator that can generate 225 trillion quatrains. Entitled *Sea and Spar Between*(11), their work combines fragments from Emily Dickinson and Herman Melville and contains the potential to create 225 trillion different quatrains, each specified by a pair of coordinates between 1 and 14992383. Montmort and Strickland utilized a JavaScript program to implement *Sea and Spar Between.*

While inspired by Montmort and Strickland's project, when it came to creating MDR's poetry generator aspect, I wanted the process to be manual. I did not want any distancing between the poet and the words. In this case, reading through my prior 27 poetry collections to create the "I forgot _____" lines meant that my subjective "I" was fully and personally involved in the creation of such lines. In other words, despite the potential randomness of line combinations to create new poems, the new poems do not eliminate authorship because of how the lines were created.

I thought it important that there be no disavowing or distancing of authorship from the work, an element I consider important as a member of a formerly colonized group as well as a poet of color in the United States. There are enough forces (from gatekeeping to racism) and would-be aesthetic trends (e.g. "the author is dead") that would erase the subjectivity of poets (and other artists) of color. Identity may ever be in flux, but the "I" always exists. Without that "I" the speaker does not exist. Without the speaker, the concerns of a poet throwing off colonial shackles or a poet of color would not exist.

But is it even possible to even write all of the poems possible through the MDR without resorting to a computer? And if so, would it even be possible to read all of them? The answer relates to the beautiful concept of Kapwa Poetics' "sacred time." In that space where time has collapsed into one, making all things one, there can exist all of the poems that can ever be written through MDR. What a magnificent possibility, made possible by Kapwa.

. . .

Finally, I am conscious that one can participate in my MDR project only if one has a copy or *MURDER DEATH RESURRECTION* or can otherwise access its database of 1,167 lines. Thus, perhaps poets can simply learn of or consider MDR's concept before proceeding to write poems whose lines begin with "I forgot." Such a result would be satisfactory to me, especially if "I forgot" poems become as ubiquitous as "I remember" poems. I know that many poets have written "I remember" poems, including poet-painter Joe Brainard whose notable book *I Remember* (1970) presents him recalling his childhood in a series of vignettes, each beginning with "I remember." I believe the phrase "I forgot" can be as generative as "I remember." Moreover, unlike with the phrase "I remember," the phrase "I forgot" offers a double-take perspective, since to claim "I forgot X" is to remember X. That result, too, befits poetry's nature: to be open to paradoxes, and be accepting of them.

Chapter 4

NEW STRUCTURES

As a former banker, I specialized in "project finance," a type of financing for industrial, infrastructure and other major projects such as factories, alternative energy producers that used garbage, wind, or water to produce electricity, mining operations, lumber- and paper-making facilities, and oil pipelines. Debt and equity investments are used to finance these projects that cost in the millions, if not billions, of dollars. Because banks, other lenders, and investors are paid back only from the projects' cash flow, the projects must succeed operationally after they've been built.

As a project finance provider, I had to understand industries and other topics about which I previously knew little or nothing. I had to learn sufficiently to get comfortable with risking huge sums on the transactions. As a potential lender, I rejected most project proposals as my analyses deemed them too risky.

Project finance and journalism shared challenges that attracted me: because their scopes encompassed a variety of topics and events, I rarely became bored. For instance, one never knew what might become news so that, randomly, I was introduced to issues that might not have come to my attention otherwise. Both disciplines also required analytical skills, and I loved exercising my brain in that manner. Poetry shares these elements—that, through poetry, I can address and analyze diverse topics. It's not surprising that I have affinity with conceptual poetry where the work is focused as much on the poem's underlying ideas as on the final product of the poem. This affinity also reflects my interest in the movie of poetry versus the snapshot-verse of the poem.

Project finance also taught me structuring—a skill I applied to my poetry inventions. During my banking days, I might receive proposals where the project's idea was sound, but the financial structure required structural adjustment. For example, if the project was based on inflation remaining steady at 5% a year, it would be wise to create a structure of financial reserves to hedge against inflation rising above projections. Other risks besides inflation could be currency exchange fluctuations, political risk (e.g., governments implementing unanticipated regulations), management quality at the companies, and my "favorite" for introducing me to the term, *force majeure*, or acts of God, such as extreme weather or war infringing on a project's operation.

For structuring the hay(na)ku, I had to persuade many poets (across a variety of poetic styles) to write in its form—this wasn't simple when the poetry world sometimes fractures into cliques and smaller communities based on poetic styles, cultures, and/or social interactions. But by the time I thought of the hay(na)ku, I also understood something about the poet's creative ego as well as how many poets thrive in play. Consequently, I deliberately heightened the use of the internet for spreading the word as well as encouraged variations that poets and, later, artists might make to and with the form.

The structure of the MURDER DEATH RESURRECTION (MDR) project is evident in its suggested use of its 1,167-line database and the phrase "I forgot." And the Flooid is set up with a condition precedent of a "good deed" to fuel the written verse (the Flooid is discussed in Chapter 7).

. . .

It's not easy to invent a poetry form. After more than two decades of creating poems, I've only been able to conceptualize three forms: the hay(na)ku, MDR-generated poems, and the Flooid. But between these formal inventions, I sought to create or structure new ways to present or promote poetry. With hindsight, these efforts could be categorized in two ways: promoting Asian American or Filipino/Filipino-American poetries and creating new spaces for presenting poetry.

Black Lightning

My first edited anthology was *BLACK LIGHTNING: Poetry-in-Progress* (1998). I joined the Asian American Writers Workshop (AAWW) while transitioning from banking to creative writing and eventually edited its *Asian Pacific American Journal. BLACK LIGHTNING* was created when AAWW decided to publish anthologies and presents my idea of showing various drafts to a single poem and interviewing its author as regards the drafting process. The questions ranged from predictable (but still useful) questions like "what inspired this poem?" to technical questions like "why did you insert a line-break here or use this form or change this word to another word?" Given the presence of the poem's drafts, the book may well be the first anthology of its type and is certainly the first for Asian American (AA) poets since only AA poets are featured.

Featuring only AA poets not only reflected its publisher AAWW's orientation, but also addressed how not as much attention was given to AA poets relative to white poets—an oversight with which I empathized as a Filipino-American. The anthology presents Meena Alexander, Indran Amirthanayagam, Mei-mei Berssenbrugge, Luis Cabalquinto, Marilyn Chin, Sesshu Foster, Jessica Hagedorn, Kimiko Hahn, Garrett Hongo, Li-Young Lee, Timothy Liu, David Mura, Arthur Sze (who also provides an introductory essay), John Yau, and Tan Lin.

Truthfully, BLACK LIGHTNING also served me directly as a newbie poet. Given my lack of formal training in poetry—I have an M.B.A. in economics and international business, not an M.F.A. in creative writing—the book exposed me to a varied set of poetries as well as advice from master poets within the two-year period required to write the book. I also noticed how my exposure to the book's diverse poetries solidified my preference for approaches that experimented radically beyond normative or traditional poetic approaches (such as those by Mei-mei Berssenbruge, Kimiko Hahn, Arthur Sze, and John Yau).

The anthology would come to be distributed by Temple University Press, partly because it became a college textbook—a result that certainly tickled me as a self-educated poet.

Asian American and Filipino-American Anthologies

BLACK LIGHTNING also introduced me to editing anthologies, a role that I discovered I enjoyed. To date, I've edited and/or conceptualized 15 anthologies of poetry, fiction, and essays. After BLACK LIGHTNING, my early anthologies included THE ANCHORED ANGEL: Selected Writings by José Garcia Villa (1999); this book won the PEN Oakland Josephine Miles Literary Award for reintroducing his poems long before Penguin Classics would release his oeuvre to the global publisher's larger audience with Doveglion: Collected Poems (2008). I then co-edited with Nick Carbo BABAYLAN: An Anthology of Filipina and Filipina

American Writers (2000). *BABAYLAN* may be the first anthology of Filipina and Filipina American writers and is significant for redressing how prior publications of Filipino writers were male-centric. I next served as poetry editor for the anthology *SCREAMING MONKEYS: Critiques of Asian American Images,* edited by M. Evelina Galang (2003), recipient of the 2004 Gustavus Myers Outstanding Book Award in the Advancement of Human Rights and ForeWord Gold Award's Best Anthology of the Year; the book was borne out of the racist incident of a restaurant review referring to a Filipino child as a "rambunctious little monkey." My next anthology was a book edited by Nick Carbo but which I conceptualized: *PINOY POETICS: A Collection of Autobiographical and Critical Essays on Filipino and Filipino-American Poetics* (2004).

Meritage Press

I didn't just conceptualize *PINOY POETICS,* which featured rare poetics presentations by Pinoy poets, but also formed a new publishing company for it. By then, I'd become aware of the difficulty of not just finding publishers but finding publishers for Filipino-related work. I ran Meritage Press from my kitchen table from 2001 to 2021. But while it published *PINOY POETICS,* the press' focus was not only Filipino authors. I didn't want *PINOY POETICS* and the other Filipino poets I published to be presented by a "Filipino press." I wanted Meritage Press to be a literary and arts press because I wanted Filipino-authored books to be contextualized within the general category of literature. I thought this would be more respectful to the quality of the works, rather than present them within the confines of Filipino literature, a category that—to be realistic—might also cause potential readers to dismiss them.

Meritage Press also reflected my desire to create new spaces for poetry and art. Befitting its desire to expand poetry's landscape, its first publication was a collaboration between poet John Yau and Archie Rand, *100 More Jokes From the Dead* (2001). John's text and Archie's images document a humorous and subversive approach to the etching medium while addressing notions about artistic approaches. The book's images were created simultaneously without revision, thus questioning the notion of etching as an art of refinement. In considering their collaborative process, Yau quotes Frank O'Hara's statement, "You have to go on your nerve alone."

In addition to presenting innovative content, Meritage Press also sought to present first-time book or chapbook publications by poets. I've been honored to publish inaugural collections by Sean Tumoana Finney, Tamiko Beyer, Ernesto Priego, Tom Beckett, Bruna Mori, Michelle Bautista, Aileen Ibardaloza, Jean Vengua, and Karen Llagas. I've also been blessed to publish books by poets who deserved more recognition, such as Barry Schwabsky, Garrett Caples, Luis H. Francia, William Allegrezza, Sheila E. Murphy, Thomas Fink, Maya Diablo Mason, Brian Clements, and Allen Bramhall. Many of these poets have gone on to publish more as well as enjoy heightened literary reputations.

Review Journals

In living as a poet, I observed how the challenge of spreading poetry went beyond writing and publishing. Poetry books often end up languishing after their releases, not just in sales but in reviews and other exposure. Thus, I created *Galatea Resurrects (A Poetry Engagement)* that presented reviews and other responses (which I called "engagements") to poetry books, poems, and other poetry-related projects. I didn't expect that *Galatea Resurrects* would last as long as it did—from 2006 to 2018—but its duration testified to its need. Indeed, further attesting to its value was how well-established critics and scholars were willing to appear for free alongside first-time critics and even children. I also published children if they gave me a response to a poem, even if the response was a drawing—one can't start too soon with introducing poetry to young people!

Relatedly, in 2015 I created *The Halo-Halo Review* (HHR) which is still ongoing. While *Galatea Resurrects* was open to addressing all writers, HHR focuses on Filipino writers around the world. My desire to promote Filipino literature will continue for as long as this specific need exists, and it still does. HHR presents reviews, features, and interviews. As with *Galatea Resurrects*, HHR also presents online reprints of such writings available only through print media—internet publishing, after all, widens the potential audience, as was proven with the hay(na)ku.

. . .

What my projects share in common is how I didn't rely on existing literary infrastructure. I developed new ways. There's a saying, *Write what you want to read.* In a similar approach, I promoted what I felt deserved to receive more attention.

This, too, is a lesson I learned from Philip Lamantia who, after all, knew much about being true to one's self. Born in San Francisco to Sicilian immigrants, Philip helped shape the Surrealist and Beat movements in the United States and has been called "the most visionary poet of the American postwar generation." During my first summer in San Francisco after moving from New York City in 1999, I had the pleasure of spending much time with him. For Philip, I wrote a reverse hay(na)ku poem entitled "How I Learned to Draw a Circle." In the poem, I wrote:

> And when you
> complained over
> your
>
> inability to draw
> a straight
> line
>
> he insisted, "Then
> draw a
> curve!"

I could have changed the poem's "you" and "your" to "I" and "my" since I was addressing myself. In refusing to abide by inherited structures including language, I was trying to be my authentic self, something Philip understood at a young age. His poetry was first published in *View* magazine in 1943, when he was fifteen. A year after appearing in the Surrealist publication edited by artist and writer Charles Henri Ford and writer and film critic Parker Tyler, Philip dropped out of Balboa High School to pursue poetry in New York City. I admire the courage and self-awareness he had at such a young age!

While I turned to poetry much later in life, I am grateful I was able to do so. Even more, I am grateful that I was able to find my own footing within Poetry's ever-shifting landscape.

Chapter 5

THE POETIC NOVEL

The creation—invention—of ways for presenting poetry affected how I decided to publish my own poems. I love being published in journals' inaugural issues because they represent an expansion of poetry spaces. I cherish being the first author published in print by xPress(ed), a publishing project curated by Finnish poet Jukka-Pekka Kervinen. Prior to my printed book *Ménage à Trois With the 21st Century* (2004), xPress(ed) was an online publishing forum. After expanding to print, Jukka came to create other print book publishers such as gradient books and, with Peter Ganick, Blue Lion Books. The latter is special for releasing poetry books with 250-plus pages (including my 400-page *SILENCES: The Autobiography of Loss*, 2007), thereby critiquing the slimness of poetry books which dominate poetry book publishing (most contemporary poetry books don't exceed 100 pages). Such length, to me, relates more to the capitalist viewpoint of poetry books: most suffer from limited sales. But this market valuation of poetry books is unrelated to aesthetic integrity. Why couldn't poetry books be massive (if that's what the work requires) just because many poetry books may not allow publishers to recover their costs? I interrogated this point of view with a book that my publisher Marsh Hawk Press nicknamed a "brick": the 504-page *I Take Thee, English, For My Beloved* (2005). (In 2007, I would release the 366-page collection *The Light Sang As It Left Your Eyes: Our Autobiography*, and this same publisher would nickname it "son of a brick," but I digress . . .)

With *I Take Thee, English, For My Beloved*, I wanted to critique the structure of most poetry books. It is not just longer than most poetry books but features 24 blurbs in front of its title page, which was something I'd seen mostly for "established" and male poets. I wasn't an established, male poet, but wanted to diss that format of privileging. Later, the publisher's book description became:

I Take Thee, English, for My Beloved contains and melds the forms of poem, memoir, art monograph, play, novel and questionnaire. Here are four discrete collections that would stand on their own but which, together, form the vibrant expanse of a book that affirms: not only does Eileen R. Tabios speak English, but she loves English. This collection is a "quar(quin)tet" partly because it contains a hidden (fifth) book—that book referenced by the series "Footnote Poems." The texts which generate the footnote-poems are not included, thus enabling a space where the readers play the roles of speculating what story(ies) is(are) being footnoted. This reflects Tabios' belief that a poet may begin a poem, but the reader completes it. The structure also manifests the paradox of how poems by themselves cannot capture the significances of Poetry as experience: that this book's true page count, like Poetry's expanse, is not fixed and, thus, is infinite.

The book description continued as follows:

Although Tabios' first poetry collection received the Manila Critics Circle National Book Award for Poetry in the Philippines, where she was born, she has lived for over three decades in, and is a citizen of, the United States. The initial impetus for this collection stemmed from her meditations on being fluent in only one language—but a language that colonized her birthland and about which she is still asked the question by strangers as she travels throughout North America: "Do you speak English?" This bespeaks the consistent "Other"-ing experience imposed by many on people of color, even second- or third-generation Americans. Nonetheless, Tabios—a "transcolonial" poet— refuses to allow adverse socio-political elements to deter her from what she feels she must do as a poet, particularly as a poet of eros: to love her raw material of English. From such love, she not only crafts poems denoting a unique vision, but writings that transcend inherited literary forms. Tabios considers the term "transcolonial" to describe a postcolonial perspective that goes beyond the referenced context of colonialism. One result is the "hay(na)ku," a poetic form which Tabios invented as a community-making gesture; here, the community encompasses both Filipino and non-Filipino poets gathered through a love of Poetry. This collection features the first publication of "The Official History of the Hay(na)ku." This collection ends with a close reading by respected poet Ron Silliman of one of Tabios' poems. Silliman concludes, "Tabios tries for more in one page than many other poets would attempt in 20. And she pulls it off."

Trying for a lot, to paraphrase Ron Silliman, reflects my deeply rooted defiance of language as a colonizing tool. Colonialism privileges the colonizer and I have no doubt that my defiance influenced my decision to write another book, *Witness in the Convex Mirror* (2019). This book honors John Ashbery with 119 poems from a series of poems that all begin with 1-2 lines from his long poem "Self-Portrait in a Convex Mirror." While my book is an homage, I also wanted to write a book that could stand proudly next to his collection *Self-Portrait in a Convex Mirror* (1975) that won the Pulitzer Prize, the National Book Award, and the National Book Critics Circle Award—the only book to have received all three awards. That John Ashbery is a master poet made him, for me, a symbol of English-language poetry and, as a Filipino-American poet, I wanted to write poems facing him instead of looking up to him. *Witness in the Convex Mirror* is one of my favorites among all my poetry collections. Here's the opening poem to my book whose first 14 words come from John Ashbery's magnificent poem; in my poem here, I wanted to have my linguistic defiance meet poetic love:

WITNESSED IN THE CONVEX MIRROR: SONG OF SPACE

We set out to accomplish and wanted so desperately
to see come into being our corralled chords
disciplined into the sublime—it is otherwise impossible
to heighten cathedrals into a space where supplicants
will feel their smallness, thus, comprehend they are not
gods. When I was young, I railed at this attempt by
architects (usually bearded men—no surprise!) who, it
seemed to me, conspired to lock humanity on the same
terrain populated by insects—bugs whose span of
the universe logically matches the tiny scale of their
bodies. Years passed and I woke up on a bench sleeping
amidst others who'd crawled in during the night seeking
solace from the freeze outside. I opened my eyes to

a rainbow settling itself upon my chest. I looked at this
odd light and whispered, "I'm no pot of gold, dear
Parmigianino." Creaking, I sat up, looked around, then
stood to approach what called me: a massive marble
altar festooned with candles, lit and unlit, fat and
thin, and in varying stages of meltdown. I was, I admit
also attracted by a nearby cart of free coffee with
milk. Above me, the altar, and the make-shift break-
fast loomed a stained-glass window from where
sunrays had entered then descended as a rainbow
that woke me. I looked at the window where someone's
son smiled with a love unfamiliar in the alleys familiar
to me. And in turning my gaze heavenward (as it were)
I felt again the largeness of the space created by a
cathedral that rose to meet its God. Thus, did I realize
the error of my youth: art—especially masterpieces—
elevate humanity. For no art was possible without
human ambition—that audacity and grace—that spares
us from the fate of our insect brothers and sisters. At
such a moment, there was nothing else to do but for me
to put down the Styrofoam cup, part my lips, raise chest
toward the hidden angels, and break into song. My chords
were disciplined. My chords were strong. I sang, and
my ambitious voice filled the massive cathedral space
into capacity. I came into being, capacious and singing

. . .

The Poet's Novel

Someone is writing a novel.
A novel is being written.
The novel is writing its author.

—from Eileen R. Tabios' novel-in-progress,
Clandestine DNA

From interrogating and expanding forms and structures within poetry,
I came to consider genre categories that would make poetry itself an

Other. I turned my attention to the form known as the "poet's novel" or "poetic novel." What would a novel look like if it were written *poetically*? After many years focusing on poetry (with only occasional forays into fiction, mostly through the short story), I decided to return to the long-form novel with which I'd begun my creative writing career. Long steeped in poetry, I was not interested in writing the way many novels are written—by telling a story conceived by its author. I thought instead: what if, instead of having an idea for a story, I let the world write my novel?

By "world" as author, I mean I believe my job as a writer is to educate myself about as much of the world as possible, whether or not I'm interested in the topics I'm learning. My job as a writer is to manifest education for education's sake, or knowledge for knowledge's sake. When it's time for me to put pen on paper—or fingers to keyboard—to write, hopefully, I would have done my job well enough so that I can be a good root source for information to apply to poems and the novel. In poetry, the approach can create fresh metaphors. In the novel, the story becomes deeper and more wide-ranging. In both cases, the work is not (unduly) limited by the limits of my imagination, including conscious interests.

I kept considering the question:

> *What if, instead of having an idea for a story, you*
> *decide to let the world write your novel?*

This approach worked for me and resulted in the 2021 release of my first novel: *DoveLion: A Fairy Tale for Our Times* from the innovative arts house publisher, AC Books helmed by artist-poet Holly Crawford. *DoveLion* came to be translated into Filipino by fictionist-scholar-translator Danton Remoto and will be published in the Philippines with the title *KalapatiLeon*. It will be released by the oldest continuing press in Asia, the University of Santo Tomas Publishing House.

Replacing myself with the "world" as author was a familiar approach when I began writing *DoveLion* on January 1, 2016. As a poet, I've long wanted to write past the limits of my imagination and, thus, was accustomed to starting a poem with no idea of how that poem would end. Often, I began with a word sparked by some feeling, and from there just wrote until the poem ended itself. "The poem ended itself" reflects a not uncommon saying among poets of how, at times, "a poem writes itself." I believed novels and poems share, or can share, something in common. If their authors are lucky, at some point during the act of writing, the work starts to write itself. This phenomenon occurs only through the writing process. Writers hope for this effect because it means that what's being written takes on a sufficiently well-developed life such that it generates its own momentum. At that point, the author becomes a tool for the work to unfold, rather than that the work progresses based on authorial guidance.

While poetry is my ideal form for best manifesting the paradox of loving a language and yet desiring to change it, I never stopped longing for the novel. I didn't consider that form lost to me because I became a poet. For, as a poet, I created in multiple genres besides the verse poem— from asemic visual poetry to experimental prose to public performances to poetry sculptures . . . and several failed attempts at the novel. When my novel drafts failed to reach completion, I usually excised the better chapters to turn into stand-alone short stories (in the process, I released 2 short story collections, *Behind the Blue Canvas* (2004) and *PAGPAG* (2020). My floundering attempts at the novel mostly remained invisible to the world; publicly, I was a prolific writer and today can point to over 70 collections of poetry, fiction, essays, and experimental biographies from publishers in ten countries and cyberspace.

But, with hindsight, I realized that I was building up a frustration over my failure. Unsuccessful with the long-form novel, I assigned myself "short novels" in 2009 and generated 12 seven-chapter novels that became my book *SILK EGG: Collected Novels 2009-2009* (2019). The mischief of *SILK EGG*'s subtitle hid my disappointment over my inability to create a longer novel. In 2019, I released a Selected Visual Poetry collection of works from 2001-2019 entitled *The Great American Novel* (2019), whose cover featured a red Valentine's Day box of chocolates in a trash can. I was reminding myself that no matter how many books I published, I had not successfully created the long-form novel.

Two decades after I began my writing career by rejecting my first completed first draft of a novel, I took a deeeeeeep breath, and assigned myself my first New Year's Resolution. I decided that for 2016 I would begin and end a novel. I resolved that I would write every day on the novel—it could be one word or 10,000 words, but I had to write daily. I wasn't concerned about word count. I was concerned about maintaining focus for which I thought even one word would do because to write one word entailed thinking about the novel. I didn't want my focus to falter over the prolonged period of a year.

Before January 1, 2016, it had been some years since my prior novel attempt. As such, I didn't have a particular idea for my novel's tale. That's when I fell back on my experience as a poet. With no story idea in mind, I thought of a phrase that begins numerous stories around the world and determined that it would begin every day's writing effort: "Once upon a time..."

That decision, as well as the goal that the novel had to be finished in one year, reminded me of constraints-based writing and specifically, Oulipo, founded by Raymond Queneau and Francois Le Lionnais. Oulipo's member of writers and mathematicians created structures and patterns for making new works. Queneau once called Oulipians "rats who construct the labyrinth from which they plan to escape."

For the novel, I determined I needed another constraint besides beginning each daily writing with "Once upon a time." One of the paradoxes of constraint-based writing (and constraints in other contexts) is how limits can enhance freedom. While freedom is desired by creatives, too much can have a deleterious effect by creating a void in which the artist/writer might flounder. I often think of Baudelaire observing how skyscrapers help facilitate the imagined wide span of the sky, because the edges of the buildings through which the sky is discerned make the image more inhabitable by the witness. I thought two constraints would be more helpful than one as I imagined myself exercising freedom but within the scaffolding of two points that would stabilize my efforts.

As I thought about what could form the second constraint, I recalled that my first efforts at the novel took place in New York City, long before I moved to my current residence of Napa Valley. I decided my second constraint would be for each section to feature the primary protagonist coming out of a Manhattan subway station, which is to say, leaving the underground darkness to come out into daylight. Obviously, I was hoping that the novel long held within me would finally surface. Or as an early sentence in the novel states:

"Once upon a time, I left dimness to break out into light."

Since 2016 was a leap year with 366 days, the novel became fashioned from 366 sections which all begin with "Once upon a time." In subsequent editing, the sections were shaped into 25 chapters. Eight chapters begin with the protagonist leaving a New York City subway station before subsequent sections moved to other introductory contexts, from "an emerald island set atop a sapphire ocean," to old age, to "a child who was insignificant to the machinations of the power-hungry," among others. Nonetheless, all sections start with "Once upon a time" and influence the novel's subtitle to reference "Fairy Tale." None of these developments occurred from (my) authorial intent. The story unfolded as it did because that's what the "world" wanted.

In *DoveLion*, for one example, educating myself about trans culture resulted in incorporating Lakapati, an indigenous transgender god of fertility and agriculture from Tagalog mythology. *DoveLion*, indeed, is published with 15 pages of notes and acknowledgements, reflecting my pre-writing job of education for education's sake. Many of these notes do not reflect research done directly for the novel but were elements that later became incorporated into the novel as its writing unfolded.

As I look at the novel's notes, I identify aspects I'd learned but not initially intended for the novel: flamenco, cataract surgery, Christian Loboutin's red-soled high heels, Kazemir Malevich's black squares, Filipino psychology, Madeleine Knobloch (Georges Seurat's long-anonymous mistress), development strategies for young nations, "pagpag" as the practice of scavenging food from garbage dumps, Randy Dudley's superb paintings, U.S. foreign policies, Kali martial art, the Romanian orphan crisis, shibari (a Japanese bondage technique), various diamond clarities, the inspiring movie *Das Leben der Anderen (The Lives of Others)* written and directed by Florian Henckel von Donnersmarck, dictatorships, the dark side of beauty pageants, and so on. I love how the list reflects the diversity of what exists in the world. It is that diversity that I wish to author my writings and for which I must always work to enable by maximizing my education on anything and everything.

Today, when I consider my publisher's book summary for *DoveLion*—

> Poet Elena Theeland overcomes the trauma of her past to raise a family who overthrows the dictatorship in Pacifica. She is aided by artist Ernst Blazer whose father, a CIA spy, instigated the murder of Elena's father, a rebel leader. As her family frees Pacifica from the dictator's dynastic regime, Elena discovers herself a member of an indigenous tribe once thought to be erased through genocide. The discovery reveals her life to epitomize the birth of a modern-day "Baybay" modeled after the "Babaylan," an indigenous spiritual and community leader of the Philippines.

Unfolding through lyrical and spare vignettes as well as the disruption of linear time, *DoveLion* presents the effects of colonialism and empire, while incorporating meditations on poetry and poetics, art and aesthetics, history, orphanhood, and indigenous values and tribal citizenships. Glimpses are provided of spy warfare, internet-based rebellions, and the insidious effects of beauty pageants. Relief is provided through Elena's love of Wikipedia and the world's most simple but delicious recipe for adobo. Ultimately, *DoveLion* bespeaks the unavoidable nature of humanity: a prevailing interconnection that can cancel past, present, and future into a singular *Now.*

—I marvel over how my 300-page novel was birthed from simply the idea of repeatedly using the phrase "Once upon a time" and seeing how many ways the phrase can engender some meaning or tale. That phrase was a portal to the world, which is much larger than myself and, thus, would be the author I would prefer for creating my works. It's a strategy reflecting what many artists and writers know: the work is larger than one's self. So why not be an author larger than one's self? Unlike a colonizer, I wanted to release control over the subjects at hand: words.

Chapter 6

THE TRAUMA ROOTING
MY LANGUAGE

The world suffers in many ways—from environmental damage to poverty to oligarchism to wars and terrorism to colonialism and its long-lasting effects. Living in such a world, any grief I feel is underpinned by my beginnings, my *roots*. I was born in the province of Ilocos Sur, Philippines. Next door in Ilocos Norte, the dictator Ferdinand Marcos, Sr. was born. Even after his ejection from his 14-year Martial Law rule, the Marcos clan retained and continues to wield a major influence in the Ilocoses. Then, in 2022, the Marcoses returned to power with the son Ferdinand Marcos, Jr. becoming the new president of the Philippines. What a huge disappointment. While the Philippines has been beset by corrupt and/or incompetent politicians, the return of the Marcoses was uniquely significant—for me, it affirmed the Philippines' failure in nation-building after World War II. How could Filipinos return the scion of a family whose policies had aborted so much potential for the country's positive development? Growing up in the Philippines during the 1960s, I still remember the optimism in the national air—we were poised to become as great as Japan whose rapid growth from 1945 to 1991 is known as the "Japanese Economic Miracle." Indeed, some thought we would exceed Japan's success given our advantage of fluency in the global language of English.

My family left the Philippines about a year before Ferdinand Marcos, Sr. declared Martial Law. Human rights abuses unfolded as his reign targeted political opponents, student activists, journalists, religious workers, farmers, and others who fought against his dictatorship. Some of his murder victims were tortured and mutilated before their bodies were dumped in various places for the public to discover—a tactic for sowing fear and which came to be known as "salvaging." Meanwhile, the Guinness Book of World Records assigned Marcos, Sr. the charge of having created the "Greatest Robbery of a Government" for his actions that included taking over companies and with a total pillage estimated from US$5 to 10 billion.

For most of my life, I had thought—and decried—how I shared a September 11 birthday with Marcos, Sr. I remember being pained when "9/11" became associated with Al-Qaeda's attacks on New York City's World Trade Center towers (where I had worked for over three years in my former banking profession), and inevitably recalling the date's association as well with the Philippine dictator. Marcos' legacy was not something I could leave behind, such that it also infiltrated my poetry. Here are excerpts from an early prose poem that burst out of me almost whole in its first draft. The title refers to Baguio City where I'd lived for most of my childhood in the Philippines:

· · ·

MY CITY OF BAGUIO

Twenty-six years later, "Baguio City" are merely two words.
Was there ever a house atop a mountain circled by an asphalt
ribbon winding its way through happiness? Was there ever a
husband, wife, eldest son, middle son, youngest son and middle
daughter who was myself as a girl? Was there a housekeeper
one pitied for a face so unappetizing she even would swallow
an eight-year-old girl's insults? Was there an eight-year-old who
was so arrogant she judged others as ugly? Does the former
eight-year-old really believe childhood bore no fraying edges?
(Was there ever a middle son who died too soon?) Was there
really a Baguio City? Ferdinand Marcos: how you confuse me!

·

Years later, in a country replete with skyscrapers, I plunge
deep into my heart and recall with awe how I never noticed my
mother pinching pennies—rather, centavos. Why did I only
have one doll? Why was she naked until my mother told one of
the servants to sew her a dress from an old t-shirt? *Servants*—
is that why I never noticed how often I ate rice with sugar
and diluted milk? Because there were always people around
sufficiently worse off that I could never do enough to make
them stop brushing my hair one hundred times an evening?

I felt unaccountable relief at pulling that dress over my doll, smoothing the fabric down past its knees. Why did I never learn to stop asking for more? I did not learn until after my departure that lesser developed countries fertilize strange ironies: when a country is too poor, even the poor have servants and this natural chain can regress forever until one might as well be an amoeba.

.

My mother frequently took me to see movies in downtown Baguio. *Just the girls*, I can hear her say in my memory, although I know that in reality, we were silent as we passed through the door, leaving behind my father equally silent as his dark eyes watched my mother's receding back. In the movie theater, I would watch my mother's legs instead of the torn screen whose stories about blonde characters never folded themselves around my kayumangi heart. I would watch her thighs—how, as she crossed her right leg over her left and, sooner or later, vice versa—her skirt would ride upwards. In the darkened theater, her stockinged thighs would gleam. I would pull her skirt down as much as I could until she pushed away my hands in irritation. Then I would content myself with looking about fiercely at who might dare notice my mother's gleaming thighs. Until my mother pinched me and whispered, *Stop fidgeting*. Then I would settle back into the same rigidity that turned my father back home into a statue. Except for my eyes—like my father's—flickering, watching for what shape the devil next would come in.

.

Black feathers, corn kernels so young their whiteness blinds, an unraveled sleeve, a weeping servant, my father's 30-inch waist, younger brother begging me to decipher a fish head, boiled bone marrows, rhinestones in my mother's eyeglasses, middle brother learning global geography by filling notebooks with foreign stamps, neighbors peeking through the fence, slices of green mango encrusted with salt, oldest brother practicing opera to the household's bated breath. *AND* behind an armchair, I sat silently, a useless doll clutched to my chest, suckling one thumb in my mouth.

.

Truly, I was a stupid child. How could I ignore any significance to the placement of my family's house atop a mountain. The views were munificent with magnificence—beyond the living room window one could stare into God's bedroom. Drop a gaze and one could consider the edges of the universe unraveling the suture against a godless black hole. The breathlessness of seeing! Such sheerness! Except for that shock interrupting the path from the bottom of the mountain up to the gates that opened onto my family's front yard stuffed with bougainvillea bushes. Halfway up and halfway down the mountain, a box leered with peeling paint, broken shutters, a mistress with a voice like fingernails scraping a blackboard and two humongous black dogs with snouts as long as a dictator's lie. I felt such relief at being attacked by those dogs. I had waited so long for the inevitable. But my family never moved from the view into God's bedroom, despite my bandages continuously sprouting red blooms whose petals insisted on widely unfurling. Just when one heard God opening his curtains, a man in Manila mugged the country we shared. Then and only then did we leave that house atop a mountain. Did we overlook so much as we tilted our eyes upward? Like the ants whose nibbles irritated dogs or distracted my family from earthly issues? Like how children define "HOME"?

.

The house next door has been occupied by a new family. It comes with a spoiled son. He was also the youngest and only male among six siblings. After thirty years of being spoiled, he is a circle of a man with a dim and depthless belly. *Baboy*—that's his nickname from the neighborhood kids. *Baboy*. Pig. All this was of no concern at first; when *Baboy* arrived, I was engrossed in collecting labels off canned goods produced by Marigold Company. For each ten labels, they would donate one centavo to my school. The nuns unleashed their whips. The principal, Sister Gloria Mantulukikulan, hectored us every morning through loudspeakers over the campus plaza where we lined up before filing into class. "Let us help Marigold Company finance new textbooks, children!" Sister Gloria's nose was red with her passion. "Yes, Sister!" our voices would float like balloons. My neighbor, *Baboy*, salivated over Linda, a sixteen-year-old maid

Mama hired out of charity. *Pssst! Pssst! Baboy* consistently called
through the fence when I had to walk by. *Maganda! Who is your
pretty sister? Baboy* would query, his snout driving through the
chain-link fence as he pushed his chin towards the direction of
Linda washing my mother's underwear while enjoying the sun. I
dutifully ignored him until he whispered, "I have Marigold labels
for you." I introduced them, pinching Linda and ordering her
to be polite as she reluctantly accompanied me to the fence. In
the aftermath, I consoled myself that at least Linda will never
starve. Then things finally died down a bit and people stopped
gossiping about how a young girl was compromised enough to
marry *Baboy*. From such small beginnings, much can and did
occur. This, after all, is a tale of hunger. There must be a reason
why, two years later, Ferdinand Marcos successfully proclaimed
Martial Law. And, now, an adult, I can't even comfort myself
by the thought of new textbooks for my childhood school—
those history books apparently have their facts all wrong.

.

Twenty-six years later I am surprised by an old Filipino. He tells
me that what I long assumed to be barbaric was actually a sign
of sophistication. Nor was it unleashed as a means to extend a
finite family budget since the practice actually was expensive.
To think I sniffed my nose at it, only once allowing—the portrait
of condescension—that its skin, at least, tasted okay after its
fur was scraped off and then charred for three hours over a
backyard fire. I don't believe I've ever tasted its ears, though I
imagine the squatters against our backyard fence must have
loved them pickled in vinegar and black pepper. It is fortunate
that my husband detests cats; I tell him I need one in exchange
for a dog he would love to have. Stalemate. I learned to tell the
difference between food and a pet. But when I left Baguio to
become an American, I left two behind: Brownie and Tigre. I
must have known their fate—even though I let the word out in
the neighborhood that I would return as a ghost to haunt them if
they ate my dogs. What I had not realized was that some might
mistake Imelda Marcos as my ghost. So the neighbors ate them
anyway, in retaliation for Imelda and her husband tightening the
means for an honest livelihood. I never thought Brownie and

Tigre would roast over a spit. But then, I never thought a greedy man would turn my birthland into a classic banana republic because the downtrodden would be unable to afford anger.

.

I recall the rains. Baguio is pronounced "bag-yo." And the Ilocano word, agbagyo, means "to storm." I recall traversing streets under an umbrella held over my neat pigtails by one of our maids. I often ducked out to quench a thirst—it was a mystery why my throat was parched by the sight of so much water!—only to be unslaked by those fat drops that loved to evade my opened lips. And I would try to satisfy myself by watching the rain slip-slide down my legs. Afterwards, Baguio City would be green and smell green. And the best part was watching the stall-owners return to Baguio City's open market. They would greet each other as if they hadn't seen each other just an hour or so before. And some would pat me on the head as we waited patiently for them to put their wares back out on display. Others would slip me candy, hushing the maid's faint protests. Soon, my cheeks would bulge like my eyes at the sight of rebirth. Overhead, the sky would become blue, as it unfailingly did after every storm over Baguio City ended.

> *Ferdinand Marcos—your red rivers stained more than 7,000 islands. But you couldn't reach the blue blue sky over Baguio City. And now you are dead. In Ilocos Norte, your wife has ordered you chilled in a freezing room. The stupid woman has mistaken you for Lenin. But I know you are underground. And I know it's hot down there. Ferdinand Marcos: I see a blue sky over Baguio City. It could have been the floor of your eternity. Look up now, into my dirty sole childishly stamping on your long nose. And again, know that the sky is blue over Baguio City. The horizon begins with what looks like a cloud, but I know it is the tip of an angel's wing. I hammer you, the chasm behind the suture that is my heart.*

. . .

It wasn't until my mid-forties, when my newly widowed mother moved in with me and my husband, that I learned that my birthday was not September 11. In an otherwise desultory evening conversation as

Mom prepared to go to sleep, she revealed that I was actually born on
the evening of a September 10; when they recorded my birth the follow-
ing day, the recorders forgot to adjust for the night birth. In other words,
I didn't share a birthday with either the dictator Marcos or a terrorist
attack on a city where I lived for nearly two decades! Mentally, I enthu-
siastically celebrated recovering my birth date from such ignominious
markers even as I calmly replied to Mom, "I wish you'd told me earlier."

I was devastated in 2022 when Ferdinand Marcos, Jr. became pres-
ident of the Philippines decades after his Martial Law dictator-father
left the office. The completion of this ugly circle made me feel that my
birthland no longer existed. That is, the birthland that contained a bright
future. Instead, the country had been buffeted into becoming something
different, more impoverished on many levels, something *less*.

In addition to falling prey to corrupt politics, the Philippines is not
different from other countries in seeing the widening disparity between
rich and poor. I can never consider any country "rich" when its pop-
ulation includes those who must forage in garbage dumps for food.
This unhealthy practice became known as "pagpag," a word that ini-
tially meant "to dust." I had to move away from poetry to the specific-
ity of prose to address this sorrow, and eventually brought out a short
story collection entitled *PAGPAG: The Dictator's Aftermath in the Dias-
pora* (2020). The publisher's description notes:

> "Pagpag" is the practice of scavenging through trash heaps
> for discarded food that the poor then attempts to clean and
> re-cook for new meals. Pagpag heart-wrenchingly symbolizes
> the effects of a corrupt government unable to take care of—
> indeed, abusing—its people. *PAGPAG's* stories, while not
> overtly addressing this radical torture of cuisine, relate to
> what lurks within the stew created by a dictator's actions.
> The aftermath is not always obvious like the imprisoned,
> the tortured, or the salvaged (murdered); the aftermath
> goes deep to affect even future generations in a diaspora
> facilitated by corruption, incompetence, and venality.
>
> Eileen R. Tabios wrote "protest stories" from 1995-2001
> against Ferdinand Marcos' martial law in the Philippines,
> including "Tapey" which was read for Hawai'i Public Radio.
> These stories, except for a 2019 story written as a coda,
> form her new short story collection, *PAGPAG*. As indicated

by its subtitle *The Dictator's Aftermath in the Diaspora,*
the collection presents stories from the points of view of
children brought out of the Philippines by their parents
(or other adults) in response to the Marcos dictatorship—
children who grew up watching and listening to adults
remember the homeland they left behind and who, as adults,
can more fully articulate the effect of their histories.

With the election of the dictator's son to become the Philippines' latest president, I felt as if my birthland had evaporated—that it no longer existed.

And yet.

I wondered if my reaction was disrespectful. Somewhere on the other side of an ocean, there still exists a country and a people. Surely no temporal—even if prolonged—rule by one family could decimate their beauty, their existence?

I returned to poetry to guide me. I began exploring how I might reach that space where, as I wrote in "My City of Baguio," my eyes would widen

> *at the sight of rebirth. Overhead, the sky would become blue, as it unfailingly did after every storm . . .*

Consequently, I invented the Flooid, a poem whose existence depended on the poet first doing a "good deed" on behalf of other people, on behalf of the environment, on behalf of other creatures like animals, among others. The Flooid is reportage poetry dependent on *goodness.*

Chapter 7

THE FLOOID

I married "Mr/s. Poetry" in 2005 to overcome my estrangement with language. My wedding album is the book *I Take Thee, English, For My Beloved*, whose cover features an image of me and my husband in our real-life wedding garb. Our image was inset brilliantly by poet-designer Claudia Carlson within a circular frame. The frame was created by letters of the English alphabet forming an oval. Despite initially feeling estranged from English, I ultimately accepted—married—it because the language also provides raw material for poetry.

Through poetry, I returned to English on a more loving basis—*to take English as my Beloved*. In looking around at all the elements that have damaged and are damaging our world—from colonialism to oligarchism to environmental havoc to poverty to racism to wars, among too many others—I didn't want to exercise damage by rejecting poetry's raw material of words. But I also wanted to address what are damaging our world.

Thus, I invented the Flooid, a short poem—no more than five lines—that only can be written after the poet first undertook a "good deed." Without a good deed, there is no Flooid poem.

The Flooid was introduced in my novel *DoveLion: A Fairy Tale for Our Times* (2021):

> "Written in five lines, the Flooid used to be inscribed
> on bamboo utilizing a precolonial script, the aknat. The
> Flooid is reportage-poetry and what it reports must be an
> activist exercise of "Kapwa," a value system based on the
> interconnectedness of all beings across all of time."

While the novel presents an example as a tanka (which also inspired the fictional script of "aknat," which is the reverse spelling of "tanka"), the Flooid can be written in any form not longer than a tanka—from a haiku to short free verse to a hay(na)ku to a couplet to a tercet to a monostich. The Flooid has to be short because, in *DoveLion*, it was designed to be inscribed on a piece of bamboo.

More significantly, the Flooid requires its author to first participate in an action to improve life *for others*, whether it's for the community, environment, and other "good causes." It cannot be a poem based on the author's imagination. As reportage poetry, the Flooid can only be based on an author's prior action to benefit others.

The following example is by a poet who could have participated in, say, helping neighbors protect their property from expected storms which are becoming more extreme from climate change. That poet wouldn't write the Flooid if s/he prepared their own property, but only if s/he also helped neighbors. (This poem bears a title, but the Flooid need not be titled.)

"THE GREAT GRIEF"

We'd grimly thinned trees
To prepare for winter's winds.
But the leaves still fell.
Tree limbs still broke. How did we
Come to trust preparation?

The poem's notion of grief stemmed from a statement by Norwegian psychologist and politician Per Espen Stoknes: "This more-than-personal sadness is what I call the 'Great Grief' . . . that our individual grief can actually be a reaction to the decline of our air, water, and ecology."

. . .

After the release of *DoveLion*, I wanted to introduce the Flooid to the public, even those who may not read my novel. My first in-person event presenting the form was before the Rotary Club of Napa on Dec. 8, 2021. I thought of the Rotary Club because it is a service organization with "a global network of 1.4 million neighbors, friends, leaders, and problem-solvers who see a world where people unite and take action to create lasting change—across the globe, in our communities, and in ourselves." For example, the Rotary Club in Napa Valley (where I reside) follows the motto of "Service Above Self" and has done so by supporting military veterans struggling with Post-Traumatic Stress Disorder. As an organization, I thought the Rotary Club conducts the kind of good deeds that could set up new Flooid poems.

I also thought of the Rotary Club because I wanted to involve those who don't self-identify as poets. As I did with the hay(na)ku and MDR poetry, I wanted the form to be open and inclusive to everybody, and not just those already involved in poetry. In turn, I felt the approach would bring new participants—*participants*, and not just audience members—to poetry.

That said, in my early introductions of the Flooid to the public, I also targeted community poet laureates because these poet laureates hold positions charged with spreading poetry throughout their respective communities.

. . .

The First Flood Poems

It's one thing to create a poetry form, but it's another thing to see who will accept the form by writing in it. I treasure knowing the inaugural poets for the Flooid, even as it is my hope that (like the hay(na)ku) the poetry form will spread until I wouldn't be able to keep track of all its practitioners. It's a blessing to share the first 20 poets who joined me in writing Flooid poems—I present them through poems and their associated good deeds.

The first official Flooid poem was written by Judge Philip Champlin, a Rotarian who was Napa Superior Court Judge from 1977-2000 and part-time traveling California Judge from 2001-2021. His poem is rooted in the Rotary Club's Global Polio Eradication Initiative that has eliminated the disease in most parts of the world.

GOOD WORKS

Are we handicapped when we can't walk?
Polio often robs us of mobility,
But not the ability to think and rejoice.
Can we be made whole?
Rotary International can.

After receiving that first Flooid poem, I also wrote my first:

NOVA

We chose the puppy
others would not want
Nova, most charming when asleep

My poem relates to how Covid-19 lockdowns caused difficulties for many animal shelters in managing their animal rescue programs. We decided to adopt one more dog as a result. We identified two German Shepherd dogs (GSD). One dog was well-behaved, and we would have wanted him for our family. Instead, we helped find him his adoptive family. We decided to adopt the other dog, Nova, because we knew she would be a difficult challenge for most families—a loud and frequent barker, she bears a past of being rehomed four times that made her skittish and suffer attachment issues. An inherently wonderful dog, Nova since has calmed down as she's been persuaded, we are her forever family. Unfortunately, her behavior calmed down by only two percent. We are looking forward to much more calm in the future (please please please!).

Here are the rest of the first 20 Flooid poems in the order I received them following a call on social media and some email solicitations. I present the poems with a brief explanation of their associated good deeds.

MARIANNE LYON
Poet Laureate of Napa County, CA, 2020–22

MY CANDLE

Everyday hero she was
Did not tell me   only to forget
but involved me   then   I truly learned
was a candle   consuming
herself to light the way for me

I invited 20 poets, storytellers, and musicians to gather at a newly opened Second Chance School, a school for children who had been expelled or dropped out of school. The school provides a reason for the kids to be in school and an opportunity to learn a trade. I bid guests to write and share an original poem about or for a teacher who inspired them. Attendees shared personal stories and creative songs. The poems were published by the *Napa Valley Register* and read at the Second Chance School. I was grateful for all these thought-filled stories and poems and used excerpts to create my poem.

.

LUISA A. IGLORIA
20th Poet Laureate of the Commonwealth of Virginia, 2020–22

> I put a book already read and loved
> into others' hands — the way, perhaps,
> one might say take care of this treasure
> I kept long; and whose light could only
> grow brighter as it circulates.

The 2021-22 Virginia Young Poets in the Community (YPIC) program is one of my Poet Laureate projects, with support from the Academy of American Poets and the Mellon Foundation, and in collaboration with the Poetry Society of Virginia. Twenty-four young poets, selected from a pool of applicants from around the commonwealth, created public poetry projects showing what matters most to them in our world today and how poetry is a tool for social engagement. For these young poets, I put together 24 packets, each containing a poets.org tote from the Academy of American Poets, a YPIC certificate, and a hand-picked poetry book from my personal collection.

.

SOFIA M. STARNES
Virginia Poet Laureate, Emerita

MEMORY CARE

> She may not know her husband is far closer
> Than the aide insists I tell her:
> *In the other wing, confined to bed. . . .*
> But he has died. His winter and his
> Spring as near to her as every word that misses.

When I'm not writing, editing, or mentoring, I volunteer, through

St. Bede Catholic Church, at a retirement community, which includes a memory care center. Recently, one of the women I visit lost her husband, and her children thought it best that we not tell her—so I abided by their wishes. I wonder, though, if she heard him nonetheless, nearby, whenever I left his name out of our conversation. There is presence in the absence of the beloved.

.

DOROTHY SALMON
Member of the Napa Rotary Club for over three decades
and its first woman president

1% of American have served their Country over our 20-year war

The Rotary Club of Napa took "Service Above Self"
to a new level to be there for those veterans

Even horrific violence could not silence our unconditional
love for our veterans and their caregivers

We planted a healing garden to heal our veterans and ourselves

Our garden is a symbol of faith, joy, remembrance and gratitude

I helped raise funds for the Club's annual cycling event "Cycle4Sight Rotary Ride for Veterans." The event raised funds for Enchanted Hills Camp for the Blind and The Pathway Home. The Pathway Home program was dedicated to helping returning veterans from the wars in Iraq and Afghanistan. They were afflicted with combat stress, PTSD, Traumatic Brain Injury and the difficult process of integrating back into civilian lives.

.

SARAH BROOKS
Graduate of Mills College with a Master's in English
with a focus in poetry

I walk with the children to the river
to give their young mother time to grieve.

I watch as a butterfly hovers over them,
somehow it resembles their father to me.

The daughter of my good friend, who I have known since she was born, suddenly became a widow when her children were just two and four years of age. I've spent many days and hours with them, trying to bring comfort amidst an impossibly deep pain in their lives. It made me realize how hard it is for most of us to sit with death, to acknowledge it and accept it. To be with people in their time of need and try to provide support even when we feel helpless to alleviate their suffering is as important as it is difficult.

DAVID HOLPER
Inaugural Poet Laureate for Eureka, California, 2019–21

YOU NEVER KNOW

What Sticks

During my years teaching college English, I developed a themed course in environmentalism. I remember sharing and discussing a study that demonstrated that altruism is a learned skill: it takes practice for people to be able to pull off heroic deeds. I framed it in the context of environmentalism, but I definitely used the idea of practicing, so when there is an emergency, such as someone trapped in a burning building, that you're able to do what is needed. One student, Daniel, stayed after that class and discussed this idea with me at some length in terms of global warming.

Probably ten years later I found a voicemail in my office from this same student, Daniel. He said that he'd been driving home from work and saw smoke pouring out of a barn just off the road. He pulled over to see if anyone needed help. He saw a woman climbing a ladder to the upper story of the barn and then going into the burning building. He immediately climbed the ladder and helped rescue her and both her trapped dogs. He said, "If I hadn't been there, she probably would have died, along with her dogs." As the poem's title suggests, you never know how what you teach can have a future impact on someone's life.

JIM LYON

Former president of the Rotary Club of Napa

THE BUM LEG

An elementary school teacher in Nicaragua
Alive with a bum leg
Polio as a kid
Who can help??
Rotary can.

Rotary has been working to eradicate polio for more than 35 years. The goal of ridding the world of this disease is closer than ever. Rotary has reduced polio cases by 99.9% since the first project to vaccinate children in the Philippines in 1979. Today, polio remains endemic only in Afghanistan and Pakistan. It is crucial to continue working to keep other countries polio free. If all eradication efforts stopped today, within 10 years Polio could paralyze as many as 200,000 children a year.

.

DENISE LOW

Poet Laureate for Kansas, 2007–09

UNDER THE MEYER LEMON TREE

A jar of marmalade waits
on the wicker table, a gift.

Alcohol wipes sit between us,

dear Marisha, my friend during Covid.
I pop a good bottle of pinot.

During the 2020-2021 lockdown in Sonoma County, my friend Marisha turned eighty. She had a daughter in a neighboring town, but otherwise no contacts. We had become friends at jazz concerts, as the only single women in attendance. We became much better acquainted over the couple of years, almost, of this quarantine. We shared a love of the arts, cuisine, and people's quirks—and the motivations for them. I miss these conversations during the depths of the United States political vagaries and the disease that brings so many deaths. Remaining hopeful became our mission.

.

KIM SHUCK
San Francisco Poet Laureate, Emerita

TOUCH VOCABULARY

"Work the paper back and forth a few times"
Clumsy at first she does
"Now twist it from here"
Folds collapse into order
She looks up, our eyes meet in wordless leap

I was born in the 60s and even then people growing up in the U.S. weren't learning to use our hands as much as our parents and grandparents had. We develop our visual sense in all kinds of new ways, but apart from using a mouse and various game/television/gadget controllers our sense of touch is languishing. I volunteered in San Francisco Unified classrooms for over 20 years. Most of what I taught in those classrooms was art based, but it was often also math, science, poetry or, what the early modern era would have called, natural philosophy. In my favorite classes, taught with Jilma Ortiz, I shared origami forms, some taught to me by artist Ruth Asawa during my own elementary school experience. I believe that cognition can be sparked in all kinds of ways, not just by reading or hearing. I have taught children with many different ability sets to fold paper, make paper, create books, weave baskets and dye fibers. Success had more to do with learning style than anything else. I'm probably always, on some level, teaching poetry. Poetry is experience after all.

.

LENY M. STROBEL
Poet-scholar and founder of the Center for
Babaylan Studies

COOKING AS SACRAMENT

Ham bone and beans simmer for three hours
Fungi log yields shiitake
Southern greens sauteed with garlic
Chicken adobo mellowing in the pot
Turmeric turned rice into gold

On Dec 29, two of my childhood friends and their families came for a visit. We haven't seen each other in decades. We all grew up together from elementary to secondary school. We all split afterwards and rarely spoke. When we did get together during class reunions, the friendship was always rekindled. On this particular visit, my good deed was allowing them to come to my home amid Covid anxiety, cook for them, feed them.

.

AILEEN CASSINETTO
Academy of American Poets Laureate Fellow

Sea,
Level, rises,
Spilling, into, clubhouses,

We never have a casual conversation when we talk about the rain. It's about the levee, the water cisterns, the rain garden system, all the invisible threads of homestead, sewer, seabed, watershed, and the whole damn planet, as if they mattered.

My Flooid poem is inspired by my San Mateo County Youth Ecopoetry Project where over 100 students participated in workshops and crafted poems that expressed their lived experiences of climate change and ideas for climate action. The first stanza is a hay(na)ku while the second is found poetry based on the article, "What Can the Bay Area Do About Rising Seas? East Palo Alto Has a Few Great Answers," by Kevin Stark & Ezra David Romero (*KQED*, April 22, 2021).

.

MELINDA LUISA DE JESÚS
Poet-scholar and former Chair of Diversity Studies
at California College of the Arts

FLOOID: BITTER BAD DAUGHTER, OR NOT MY JOB
TO STROKE YOUR FRAGILE BROWN EGO

long ago i made a book[1] for us[2]

but misogynist "colleagues" came for
my job, tried to silence me[3]

now fake-woke predators pretend they
were "intersectional" all along

my book's still in print as peminist works
arise joyfully throughout the diaspora

tell me again how i "didn't serve the community"

I compiled the first anthology of peminist/Filipina American feminist thought, *Pinay Power: Peminist Critical Theory* in 2005. It came about because male colleagues insisted that focus on Filipina realities detracted attention from "real problems" (aka Pinoy-defined issues). I noted same in the anthology's introduction. About 3 years after its publication, I received a cease-and-desist letter from one "Crisostomo Ibarra" (of *Noli Me Tangere!*) demanding a public apology for slander and the destruction of all remaining copies of my book. I served "Crisostomo" with the threat of a SLAPP lawsuit and never heard from him again.

Today, these men front that they've always been feminist/intersectional, denying their sexual harassment of students/colleagues, and their denigration of queer theory/folks back in the day. I hold these "educators" accountable for the pain and trauma they inflicted upon us.

All skinfolk are not kinfolk.

1 *Pinay Power: Peminist Critical Theory: Theorizing the Filipina/American Experience*, Routledge (2005)

2 See Ruby Ibarra et al's iconic "Us" (2018)

3 See my introduction to *Pinay Power*.

JOYCE PRESCOTT
Retired Human Resources consultant and
member of the Rotary Club

ROTARY CLUB OF NAPA

For third graders we provide dictionaries

For blind children and teens, we raise money for Camp

For PTSD victims of war, we invite them into our lives

For the poor and dispossessed, we ring the Salvation Army bell

Rotary cares.

Rotary Club of Napa is a group of eighty-plus members who believe in
our community and provide support to Napa Valley through a number
of projects. We believe in "Service Above Self," but the rewards of our
work are immeasurable: the smiles on third graders' faces as they open
the colorful pages of dictionaries; the joy of music and songs created
and performed by youth without sight; the ability of veterans plagued
by the horrors of war to regain their love of life; and delicious meals cre-
ated by a chef who was formerly homeless before graduating from the
Salvation Army Culinary Program. Such are the tangible results of Rota-
ry's service.

JOHN PETRAGLILA
Poet and Board Member of Napa Valley Writers

Mentoring pays off
Juan is thriving in college
Siblings think big too!

Working in downtown Oakland for 15 years, I volunteered as a Men-
tor at an East Bay College Program. I met Juan as a HS senior consid-
ering college—the first in his family! We struggled at first but slowly
bonded over halting bilingual conversations with his parents, college

and loan applications, deciding on majors and other imaginable vicissitudes. Overwhelmed a few times, Juan persevered and graduated UC Irvine on time, has a job in health care and is pursuing post graduate education. The added benefit to his success—his siblings believe this could also be their reality. This is one of 300 haiku I wrote during Covid.

.

ZVI A. SESLING
Poet Laureate of Brookline, MA, 2017–20

HER HOUSE BURNED

Her house burned in
the Glass Fire—
all lost, house, books
I sent what I could—
her books she had sent me

When the Glass Fire swept through Napa, CA, a poetry friend lost all her books—thousands of them, most importantly, all of her own books, some of which she had signed and sent to me, including, as she said, one that was, "the last copy on Earth." I sent some back to her and my reward was her happiness.

.

CHARLES CARR
Poet and host of *Philly Loves Poetry*,
a monthly broadcast on PhillyCAM

FIGHTING THE NINJAS

At a Stop light a man holds up a handwritten sign/
"Wifey killed by Ninjas, need $ for karate lessons/
I gave him an extra dollar for creativity/
Don't laugh he earned it.

I was driving my son home when we came to a stop light at a very busy and somewhat dangerous intersection before the Schuykill Expressway (South Philadelphia). We were approached by the man holding the sign and begging sincerely for money. We realized the man probably was mentally ill. But it was the most creative sign I have encountered in a city that has many homeless people begging for money.

.

MELISSA ELEFTHERION CARR
Poet Laureate of Ukiah, CA

FERAL

Rawboned & hungry, her green eyes pleading
She sauntered over, I stretched out my hand
Medicine, food, an open window
We named her "Hildegard," she only answers to "Pants."

Behind the library where I work is an alley, which is quite popular for finding feral kittens. One day, a gaunt, grey kitten with beautiful green eyes sauntered over to me & head-butted me a few times as I stroked her fur. My family & I had been looking for a new kitten to add to our furry brood of rescues, & once they met her, they were goners too. Later, I learned from a man who sometimes sleeps in the alley that she had been keeping warm in his sleeping bag with him at night but would patrol the area every hour or so to keep guard for their safety. After more than two years living with us & being part of our family, she still patrols the house & backyard, though now she has both the stability of home as well as a very strong sense of identity.

.

JOHN PRESCOTT
Retired banker and member of the Napa Rotary Club

ROTARY CLUB OF NAPA

For 102 years they met: farmers, bankers, real estate agents
Teachers, lawyers and judges, businessmen and women
They cared about their community and did projects
Raised money and hopes while they raised their community
They raised themselves.

The Rotary Club of Napa is 102 years old in 2022 and has succeeded year after year in bringing in new generations of Rotarians who care about the Napa Valley Community and the greater world community. The Club exemplifies the words of Margaret Mead: "Never underestimate the power of a small group of committed people to change the world. In fact, it is the only thing that ever has."

KACI RIGNEY
Singer, songwriter, recording artist, published poet, and aspiring novelist

> For Sale: Lovely Leather Loveseat
> Cream colored and comfy
> Minutes marked a miracle
> Sofa needed, said someone special
> It's yours, my friend. Feel free.

I volunteered at a house for recovering addicts. Kerrie, one of the first to graduate, and I became good friends. Her life choices ravaged her life, she had lost everything including her children. Since graduating, her family has been restored. As I was preparing to move, we needed a new home for our sofa. I had just posted it for sale when Kerrie posted on Facebook that she needed a couch. I messaged her right away. *I have one, my friend. It's yours!* Stroke of serendipity and satisfaction.

JOANN BALINGIT
Poet Laureate of Delaware, 2008–15

FLOOID FOR JOAN

> I found the address in a notebook
> and copied it on the post card, a Singer Sargent
> hillside in Spain to say I'd been here, nearby
> and couldn't get there, in umber shadow
> and olive leaves to meet you finally, at last.

This poem is about two things. First is trying to teach myself to love isolation less. And second, about writing and dropping into the mail, a first-time note to my sister-in-law. We haven't met in person or "on Zoom"—we found each other on Facebook a few years back and recognize the importance of our connection. A hand-written letter is an act of love.

· · ·

In *DoveLion*, the Flooid is described as being inscribed on bamboo—this relates to one of its real-life inspirations, the ambahan, a traditional poetry form by the Hanunó'o Mangyan people of Mindoro, Philippines. Ambahan was/is recorded on bamboo and inscribed in Surat Mangyan, an indigenous Filipino script. The bamboo inscription provided a natural constraint to the poem's length. While it's not necessary, I would not object to today's poets inscribing the Flooid on bamboo (or any other material). But I more emphasize making true its fictional purpose as described in my novel: that one first must do a good deed before one can write a Flooid poem. No Flooid poem can exist without its underlying inspiration of a good deed.

My latest Flooid project is my first children's book, *Tata Edgar's Forever Laughter*, with illustrator Mel Vera Cruz and psychologist Jeannie Celestial. This will be my first children's book and, of course, I won't do it the way most children's books are created. While its story can work as a stand-alone story, the book will feature an Afterword essay by Dr. Celestial on how to guide children in addressing the death of someone they know. In the Flooid spirit, it's not enough to create a literary work; I wished to create a literary work that could serve a good deed of helping children by helping them process grief. The story also incorporates seven Flooid poems based on a good deeds originating from kindness, generosity, and love for animals.

One by one. Can the accumulation of good deeds change the tenor of our hurting world? Can such mitigate abuse? Can such alleviate damage suffering? With the Flooid, I wanted to create an activist poetry form based on hope. Through the Flooid, I want to keep hoping.

Chapter 8

DEAR READER,

I love art. The visual arts' influence on my poetry can't be overstated and is reflected throughout my books. It seemed inevitable, therefore, that I'd want to support visual artists as much as poets. Specifically, I wanted to manage an art gallery on their behalf. When my son Michael left for college, I turned his playroom into such a gallery, calling it North Fork Arts Projects (NFAP) after the street where my home is located. With hindsight, I had joined a group of art lovers who turned their residences into art galleries; we surfaced in places like Berlin, Singapore, Brooklyn, Tokyo, Cambridge, Australia and, with me, Saint Helena. The trend is supported by many factors such as out-of-the-box thinking (pun intended since a gallery has been called a "box") and that it helps avoid the prohibitive expenses of gallery spaces.

For NFAP, I combined its physical space with an online presence. I augmented the art images with essays and other prose that would educate the viewer/reader about the artist's work. I focused on Filipino artists because, as with Filipino poets, I felt they needed more exposure. The gallery opened with an exhibit by Texas-based Matt Manalo in December 2018. I then opened a new exhibit almost every month. I adored my gallery project whose global impact was enabled by the internet and whose exhibitions presented paintings (Isabel Cuenca, Jean Vengua, Ulysses Duterte, Treva Tabios, and Juan Elani Tulas), mixed-media installations (Mel Vera Cruz, Cristina Querrer and Remy Cabacungan), mail art (Glynda Velasco), drawings (Leny Strobel and Karl Frederic Meneses), sculptures (Melinda Luisa de Jesus), and book art (Ivy Alvarez, Paolo Javier/Emmanuel Lacaba, Sean Labrador Y Manzano).

Then the Glass Fire occurred, one of the mega wildfires hitting the Western U.S. as the region suffered from years of drought. The Glass Fire began as a single 20-acre brush fire on Sept. 27, 2020 before rapidly burning nearly 70,000 acres in the Napa and Sonoma Counties to destroy over 1,500 structures such as residences, businesses, wineries, and historic sites. My home, too, was destroyed by fire and smoke. Nearly three years later as I write this book, I still have not been able to return to the mountain where I'd lived for nearly 20 years; instead, I reside in a temporary rental home.

Among the many things I mourned because of Glass Fire was the abrupt end to my gallery activities—there were so many more artists I would have wanted to feature. As I ended my second year as a fire refugee, I began considering how I might continue a gallery operation: I didn't feel like giving the wildfire the last word. I decided to continue NFAP at my fire evacuee residence. Given that my rental home is much smaller than my pre-fire residence, the gallery's physical space also downsized to, not even a closet but, a closet door.

My rental home contains a closet with two sliding doors. For NFAP, I aligned both doors, one behind the other. When the front door is slid away, the second closet door is revealed as the "gallery" with hanging artwork. All artworks have to be flat, since the distance between the two doors is 3/8th of an inch. It may well be the world's thinnest gallery—I may yet apply for a Guinness World Record!

I call this "branch" of NFAP "The Refugee's Art Gallery." I inaugurated it with a drawing exhibition by Ulysses Duterte. Shortly thereafter, I received commitments for six 2023 exhibitions that involve artists and poets. Despite its radically constrained space, my new gallery looks to be a success. Its new motto proclaims, *ART IS RESILIENT!*

I doubt that I would have conceptualized The Refugee's Art Gallery without a poetry practice based on creating new approaches.

. . .

In March 2022, Russia invaded Ukraine. Along with many poets around the world, I responded—had to respond—through poems. My first was a monostich to reflect how my usually verbose self was initially almost speechless at the horrors inflicted by Vladimir Putin:

KHARKIV

All roses turned grey.

On February 28, 2023, my local newspaper, *Napa Valley Register,* featured an opinion piece by Eugene Finkel, an associate professor of international affairs at Johns Hopkins University and author of the forthcoming book *To Kill Ukraine.* Finkel described Vladimir Putin's views as reflecting "a long-standing tradition of Russian historiography, nationalist thinking and official policy that views Great Russians, Little Russians (that is, Ukrainians) and White Russians (Belorussians) as different branches of a single ancient Russian people that originated in the medieval Kievan Rus state." The 2022 Russian invasion is consistent, says Finkel, with how "to ensure that Ukrainians remain nothing more than Russians' little brothers" so that "the Russian Empire and later the Soviet Union engaged in a determined campaign to suppress and, at times, physically eliminate Ukrainian cultural figures, political elites and intellectuals and even the Ukrainian language itself."

Finkel's commentary was triggering for reminding me of how, in colonizing the Philippines, the United States called Filipinos their "Little Brown Brothers." A century later, the paternalistic condescension still rankles.

Ironically, while the Russia-Ukraine war unfolded, I was invited to deliver a poetry reading through the American Center in Moscow's virtual series, "Meet a Poet" that is managed by the Forum for Cultural Engagement (FCE), a cultural diplomacy organization founded by singer-songwriter Mary McBride to produce multi-faceted, interdisciplinary programming around the world. The opportunity came with a chance for my poems to be translated for the first time into Russian. I'd previously been translated into 11 languages—the most recent were my first two French books, *Prises (Double Take)* (trans. Fanny Garin, 2022) and *La Vie erotique de l'art* (trans. Samuel Rochery, 2021). I appreciate translations for providing another path for my poems to travel throughout the universe, so I normally would have leapt at the opportunity for my poems to fly in Russian.

In response to the invitation, I raised Russia's invasion of Ukraine. FCE replied by quoting the U.S. State Department's policy of decrying Russia's invasion while also maintaining a difference between the Russian people and Putin's policy, as well as their belief that cultural exchanges can play a role in defusing tension. I decided to participate, but only by incorporating a hidden support for Ukraine among my poems. For the event moderated by AJ Odasso and with Russian translations provided by Anna Krushelnitskaya, I wrote

BANOG (KITE)

The Philippine Eagle is the Philippines' most evolutionarily
distinct and globally endangered species.
—The Zoological Society of London

Under duress,
knowing forests are
reducing themselves into
ants, the eagles
insist on washing ashore
nude without feathers
elevating their wings

Once upon a time
the Philippine Eagle
scoffed at Icarus—
the line between myth
and the 21st century
was tethered to earth
before it evaporated—

the line between myth
and the 21st century
is humanity's profile

    The first stanza is acrostic with the first letters of each line spelling out "Ukraine." I modeled my hidden protest after Pete Lacaba's poem, "Prometheus Unbound," an acrostic poem where the first letters of each line spelled out "Marcos Hitler Diktador Tuta," then a popular Tagalog slogan among those protesting the Philippines Martial Law Era (1972-1986). The poem initially seemed to be a retelling of the Greek myth involving Prometheus, a neutral topic for the times. It was only after its 1973 publication in *Focus Magazine* that the poem was revealed to be protest poetry. Similarly, I hid the Ukraine reference behind, for a Russian audience, the politically neutral concern over the endangerment of the Philippine Eagle.

    My Russia-Ukraine-related intervention may not have much impact, but I share this information for the first time through this book as part of the protests by me and other poets worldwide over Russia's Ukraine invasion. My other interventions include a folio of Filipino poets writing against Russia's invasion which I published online at *The Halo-Halo Review* in April 2022.

The war in Ukraine is, sadly, just one of many tragedies damaging our world. It is my hope that the Flooid may help ease the pressure on our planet for the encouragement it provides for creating good deeds.

This focus on good deeds manifests my evolution as a postcolonial to a transcolonial subject. I've long preferred the term "transcolonial" because I considered "postcolonial" insufficient for reflecting my desire to transcend being contextualized simply by my colonized history. I understand "transcolonial" is not a new term in academic quarters, but when I first applied it to my work more than two decades ago, I defined "transcolonial" as wanting to *trans*-cend into other concerns or interests not instigated by colonialism. As I behaved transcolonial-ly by tinkering with language, I came to something more basic and fundamental: ethics. "Being a poet is not writing a poem but finding a new way to live," said the poet Paul le Cour; while I know little about this Danish poet's work, his statement was a formative influence on me after I discovered it as a beginning poet. For "a new way to live," I'd like my poetry to make me a better person who helps lighten the world's burdens with more good deeds from the planet's most powerful species: humans.

I hope readers will join me in Poetry, even to play around like Jim McCrary, a poet based in Lawrence, Kansas and William Burroughs' former associate whose contribution reminds that invention is also *play*. Jim sent the following:

FLAWED FLOOID

ONE

GOOD

DEED

DESERVES

AN OTTER

Surely, we all love the otters whose playfulness, after all, shows another facet of poetry. In play and goodness, I invite readers to make poems. And if those poems happen to occur through or be informed by the Flooid, hay(na)ku, or the MDR Poetry Generator's encouragement to remember by articulating what you "forgot," then my own poetry would be blessed for having surfaced without the necessity of *my* words. For

Dear Reader, my poetry has never been my words, but yours.

Selected Notes & Bibliography

Proem

My 1999 summer with Philip Lamantia is among the highlights of my life. Once, he served me Portuguese wine and cheese in his apartment; my eyes were wide as I partook of his generous repast while my eyes traveled from one tall stack of books to another. Then he took me to a reading in North Beach where he introduced me to Lawrence Ferlinghetti. On another occasion, he met me and my husband for dinner at the Persian restaurant Maykadeh—he chose the restaurant because "they do wonder with tongues." Over two decades later, I would write a series of "wine country poems" based on daily walks throughout my residence of Napa Valley—each time I wrote a poem, I remembered how he had suggested that I be "a poet of place" as part of generating roots within my diaspora. Philip's inspiration continues to reverberate long after our shared summer.

BIBLIOGRAPHY:
"Proem," *Poem Analysis*, https://poemanalysis.com/definition/proem/
    "The Proem to the Aeneid," *Berean Classical Homeschool Co-Op*, https://learningtogether2012.wordpress.com/2011/09/09/the-proem-to-the-aeneid/

Chapter 1

My poetic origins in "abstract"-ed language make me empathize with Argentinian poet Maria Negroni who, coming out of the "long night" of a dictatorship and the crisis of displaced migrants, wrote poems that translator Michelle Gil-Monterey says refuse being situated in contexts to reflect the "anxiety" of "language posing a mortal threat to whatever it references." Quotes from *Exilium* by Maria Negroni, Translated from the Spanish by Michelle Gil-Monterey (Ugly Duckling Presse, 2022).

I made the joke of following in T.S. Eliot's footsteps several times in my early years as a poet. It wasn't until just recently—through an exchange with poet-scholar Joi Barrios (per a March 29, 2023 Facebook conversation)—that I realized that name-dropping Eliot's name was an unconscious colonial rationalization, exemplifying colonial and postcolonial theorist Homi Bhabha's concept of mimicry, given how colonial Filipino culture can privilege U.S.-American and/or Western culture.

BIBLIOGRAPHY:
History of Brent International School Baguio at https://brentbaguio.edu.ph/history/
    "Telling the History of the U.S. Through Its Territories" by Anna Diamond, *Smithsonian Magazine*, January 2019.
    "Are poets born, not made?" by Harriet Staff, Poetry Foundation, June 5, 2010.
    "T.S. Eliot at Lloyds Bank," tseliot.com, March 30, 2017. https://tseliot.com/foundation/t-s-eliot-at-lloyds-bank-2/
    Returning the Borrowed Tongue, Editor Nick Carbo (Coffee House Press, 1996).

REFERENCED BOOKS BY EILEEN R. TABIOS:
    I Take Thee, English, For My Beloved (Marsh Hawk Press, 2005)

Reproductions of the Empty Flagpole (Marsh Hawk Press, 2002)
Beyond Life Sentences (Anvil, 1998)
Sun Stigmata (Marsh Hawk Press, 2014)
The Great American Novel (Paloma Press, 2019)
Silk Egg (Shearsman Press, 2011)

Chapter 2
Single-author hay(na)ku collections have been written by William Allegrezza, Ivy Alvarez, John Bloomberg-Rissman, Heath Brougher, Aileen Cassinetto, Donna Fleischer, Alex Gildzen, Scott Keeney, Heikki Lahnaoja (first Finnish hay(na)ku book), Rebecca Mabanglo-Mayor, Sheila E. Murphy, Bruce W. Niedt, lars palm, Dijana Petkova (first two hay(na)ku collections in Macedonia), Ernesto Priego (the first hay(na)ku book author), Radhey Shiam (first hay(na)ku book in India), and Eileen R. Tabios.

Thirteen translators, as part of the Poetry and Translation Seminar at the National Autonomous University of Mexico (UNAM), translated 36 poets from the now out-of-print *The First Hay(na)ku Anthology*, Co-editors Jean Vengua and Mark Young (Meritage Press / xPress(ed), Saint Helena and Finland, 2005). Their translations form the second section of the anthology *HAY(NA)KU 15*, the 15th year anniversary hay(na)ku anthology, Editor Eileen R. Tabios (Paloma Press / Meritage Press / xPress(ed), San Mateo, Saint Helena and Finland, 2018). The translators are Luis Felipe Alvarez, Liliana Andrade, Argel Corpus, Maria González de Leon, Alvaro Garcia, Melisa Larios, Rebeka Lembo, Aurelio Meza, Alejandra Navarrete, Ernesto Priego, Itzel Rivas, and Alfredo Villegas.

BIBLIOGRAPHY:
Poetry Foundation Glossary of Poetic Terms: Reader-response theory at https://www.poetryfoundation.org/learn/glossary-terms/reader-response-theory
    The Hawkline Monster by Richard Brautigan (Simon & Schuster, 1974)
    Wikipedia on the word "pneumonoultramicroscopicsilicovolcanoconiosis"
    The First Hay(na)ku Anthology, Co-Editors Jean Vengua and Mark Young (Meritage Press / xPress(ed), 2005)
    "Orphan Statistics Explained" by The Schuster Institute for Investigative Journalism, Brandeis University. https://www.brandeis.edu/investigate/adoption/orphan-statistics.html
    May 23, 2023 email from Lisa Suguitan Melnick regarding the Katipunan Learning Community at the College of San Mateo

REFERENCED BOOKS BY, OR EDITED BY, EILEEN R. TABIOS:
    I Take Thee, English, For My Beloved (Marsh Hawk Press, 2005)
    Your Father Is Bald (Pim Publishing House's "Bibliotheca Universalis" Collection, 2017)
    ONE, TWO, THREE: Selected Hay(na)ku Poems, bilingual English-Spanish edition with translator Rebeka Lembo (Paloma Press, 2019)
    147 Million Orphans (gradient books, 2014)
    HAY(NA)KU 15 (Meritage Press / xPress(ed), 2018)
    To Be An Empire Is To Burn (Moria's Locofo Chaps, 2017)
    The Chained Hay(na)ku, curated by Eileen R. Tabios with Ivy Alvarez, John Bloomberg-Rissman, & Ernesto Priego (Meritage Press, 2010)

Chapter 3
"Faith" was previously published in *I Take Thee, English, For My Beloved* (Marsh Hawk Press, 2005):

FAITH

stalactites etching wooden cheeks

    statues of weeping saints
                bobbing amidst waves

            "you the unknown
            port behind distant mist"

the image of tears carving wood—of what
is this a seed?

include these "dreams by a battered mind"
inhale deeply   Breathe

To bring the poem into the world
is to bring the world into the poem

Did not St. John of the Cross muster
a great lyric poem despite "severe sensual deprivation"?

                then exhale the white light

of the North Star, constant
-ly whispering, "You can always know where you are"

      thus moving one hand to my wrist, the other to my waist

pulling me closer to lean against you, my *Wood*

            Beloved.   What respite exists
            when I search for you whom I do not know?

And Paz notes the link between Christians and Dadaists
for both "speak in tongues"

And "Harmony, the essence of music, in poetry
produces only confusion"

And we are free with each other though we cannot memorize
each other's scent   *Love as pure Form?*

And no-Self is a Self

And your mask offers what a red rose offers: reflection I recognize as my face

And _____

And _____

_____ And

BIBLIOGRAPHY:
Zombie Notes by Maureen Owen (Sun Books, 1985)
The No-Travels Journal by Maureen Owen (Cherry Valley Editions, 1975)
~~Dipstick~~ *(Diptych)* by Tom Beckett (Marsh Hawk Press, 2014)
GLIMPSES: A Poetic Memoir by Leny M. Strobel (Paloma Press, 2019)

REFERENCED BOOKS BY, OR EDITED BY, EILEEN R. TABIOS:
I Take Thee, English, For My Beloved (Marsh Hawk Press, 2005)
Others below.

NOTES ON THE SECTION "MURDER DEATH RESURRECTION":
1 "Defining Kapwa," *Babaylan Files*, April 5, 2009. http://babaylanfiles.blogspot.com/2009/04/defining-kapwa.html (Accessed Jan. 14, 2018)
2 Tabios, Eileen. *After the Egyptians Determined The Shape of the World is a Circle* (Lutherville, MD: Pometaphysics Publishing, 1996)
3 The following books and chapbooks were created by Eileen R. Tabios through the MDR Project: *44 RESURRECTIONS* (Online: PostModernPoetry E-Ratio Editions, 2014); *I FORGOT LIGHT BURNS* (Chicago: Moria Books, 2015); *DUENDE IN THE ALLEYS* (Online: Swirl Editions, 2015); *AMNESIA: Somebody's Memoir* (New York / Berkeley: Black Radish Books, 2016); *THE OPPOSITE OF CLAUSTROPHOBIA: Prime's Anti-Autobiography* (Merseyside, U.K.: Knives, Forks and Spoons Press, 2016); *THE CONNOISSEUR OF ALLEYS* (New York: Marsh Hawk Press, 2016); *EXCAVATING THE FILIPINO IN ME* (Hawai'i: Tinfish Press, 2016); *WHAT SHIVERING MONKS COMPREHEND* (Chicago: Locofo Chaps, 2017); *HIRAETH: Tercets From The Last Archipelago* (Merseyside, U.K.: Knives, Forks and Spoons Press, 2018); and *MURDER DEATH RESURRECTION: A Poetry Generator* (Loveland, OH: Dos Madres Press, 2018)
4 MDR's poem, "Excavating the Filipino In Me," was displayed as visual poetry in "Chromatext Rebooted," a visual poetry and arts show organized by the Philippine Literary Arts Council at the Cultural Center of the Philippines, Manila, from Nov. 6, 2015 to Jan. 17, 2016. The exhibition was curated by Alfred A. Yuson and Jean Marie Syjuco.
5 Baker, Alan. "*The Opposite of Claustrophobia* by Eileen Tabios, pub. Knives, Forks and Spoons Press." *Litter*. http://leafepress.com/litter9/tabiosreview2/tabiosreview2.html (Accessed Jan. 10, 2018)
6 Fink, Thomas. "Exchange with Eileen R. Tabios on her Poetics." *Dichtung Yammer*. https://dichtungyammer.wordpress.com/2017/04/26/exchange-with-eileen-r-tabios-on-her-poetics/ (Accessed Jan. 10, 2018)
7 Beckett, Tom. ~~Dipstick~~ *(Diptych)*. (New York: Marsh Hawk Press, 2014).
8 Tabios, Eileen. *Reproductions of the Empty Flagpole* (New York: Marsh Hawk Press, 2002).
9 Katrin De Guia. *Kapwa: The Self in the Other* (Pasig City, Philippines: Anvil Publishing, 2005). 4,5
10 Tabios, Eileen. "Sacred Time" in *Our Own Voice*, August 2010. http://www.oovrag.com/poems/poems2010b-tabios3.shtml (Accessed July 12, 2018)
11 Nick Montfort and Stephanie Strickland. *Sea and Spar Between in The Winter Anthology*, Vol. 3, 2011. http://winteranthology.com/?vol=3&author=montfort-strickland&title=seaandspar (Accessed Jan. 10, 2018).

Chapter 4
While noting my affinity for Conceptual Poetry, I differ from some conceptual poets by maintaining my desire to write compelling poetic lines that others would want or be interested in reading. I came across a similar idea for the visual arts when I read Jordan Eddy's article in

Hyperallergic (April 9, 2023) that presented Lucy Lippard and Lisa Le Feuvre discussing the legacy of U.S.-American artist Nancy Holt. In that article, Jordan Eddy asked Lucy Lippard why she's written that Nancy Holt "was never a Conceptual artist, per se." Lucy Lippard replied (the bracketed phrase below is mine):

> *"I have a very strict definition of conceptual, which most people don't. It gets used on absolutely everything now. It seems like if there's any idea involved it's conceptual. But in those days I was thinking it was dematerialized conceptual art, and that's why I didn't think she was one. Conceptual is really about ideas, and perceptual is about seeing [so that the art object matters]. But there's a lot of back and forth; I don't think there's a strict line between the two."*

BIBLIOGRAPHY:
Doveglion: Collected Poems of Jose Garcia Villa, Editor John Edwin Cowen with an Introduction by Luis H. Francia (Penguin Classics, 2008)
The poem "How I Learned to Draw A Circle" first appeared in *The In(ter)vention of the Hay(na)ku: Selected Tercets 1996-2019* by Eileen R. Tabios (Marsh Hawk Press, 2019).
John Yau and Archie Rand, *100 More Jokes From the Dead* (Meritage Press, 2001)
Wikipedia on Philip Lamantia

REFERENCED BOOKS BY, OR EDITED BY, EILEEN R. TABIOS:
BLACK LIGHTNING: Poetry-in-Progress (Asian American Writers Workshop, 1998)
THE ANCHORED ANGEL: The Writings of José Garcia Villa (Kaya Press, 1999)
BABAYLAN: An Anthology of Filipina and Filipina American Writers, co-edited with Nick Carbo (Aunt Lute Press, 2000)
SCREAMING MONKEYS: Critiques of Asian American Images edited by M. Evelina Galang for which Eileen R. Tabios serves as poetry editor (Coffee House Press, 2003)
PINOY POETICS: A Collection of Autobiographical and Critical Essays on Filipino and Filipino-American Poetics edited by Nick Carbo as conceptualized by Eileen R. Tabios (Meritage Press, 2004)

Chapter 5
BIBLIOGRAPHY:
Oulipo information are from Wikipedia.
Self-Portrait in a Convex Mirror by John Ashbery (Penguin Poets, 1990)

REFERENCED BOOKS BY, OR EDITED BY, EILEEN R. TABIOS:
I Take Thee, English, For My Beloved (Marsh Hawk Press, 2005)
Ménage à Trois With the 21st Century (xPress(ed), 2004)
SILENCES: The Autobiography of Loss (Blue Lion Books, 2007)
The Light Sang As It Left Your Eyes: Our Autobiography (Marsh Hawk Press, 2007)
DoveLion: A Fairy Tale for Our Times (AC Books, 2021)
SILK EGG: Collected Novels 2009-2009 (Shearsman Books, 2019)
The Great American Novel: Selected Visual Poetry (2001-2019) (Paloma Press, 2019)
Behind the Blue Canvas (Giraffe Books, 2004)
PAGPAG: The Dictator's Aftermath in the Diaspora (Paloma Press, 2020)
Witness in the Convex Mirror (TinFish Press, 2019)

Chapter 6
"Fact check: Guinness not disputing a historical fact on 'greatest robbery of
a gov't'" by Kristine Joy Patag, *Philstar.com*, March 18, 2022, provides a useful
summary of the topic of Ferdinand Marcos, Sr. being a Guinness Book World
record holder as a thief. https://www.philstar.com/headlines/2022/03/18/2168193/
fact-check-guinness-not-disputing-historical-fact-greatest-robbery-govt

REFERENCED BOOK BY EILEEN R. TABIOS:
  PAGPAG: The Dictator's Aftermath in the Diaspora (Paloma Press, 2020)

Chapter 7
REFERENCED BOOKS BY EILEEN R. TABIOS:
  I Take Thee, English, For My Beloved (Marsh Hawk Press, 2005)
  DoveLion: A Fairy Tale for Our Times (AC Books, 2021)

Chapter 8
The Zoom reading through the American Center in Moscow's virtual series, "Meet a Poet"
that is managed by the Forum for Cultural Engagement is available on YouTube.

My curated folio of Filipino poets writing against Russia's invasion of Ukraine was published
in *The Halo-Halo Review* (April 2022) and featured the poets Cynthia Buiza, Aileen Cassinetto,
Luisa A. Igloria, Marne Kilates, Eileen R. Tabios, and Alfred A. Yuson.

BIBLIOGRAPHY:
"10 homes that double up as galleries or artists' workspaces"
by Natashah Hitti, *dezeen*, Sept. 15, 2017. https://www.dezeen.
com/2017/09/15/10-home-interiors-galleries-artists-workspaces-pinterest-roundup/
  "What the world learned about Ukraine in a year of war" by Eugene Finkel, *Napa Valley
Register*, Feb. 28, 2023.
  About FCE: Forum for Cultural Engagement. https://www.fcengage.org/fceabout
  "The Marcos-era Resistance Poem that Smuggled a Hidden Message into State Media" by
Paolo Enrico Melendez, *Esquire*, Sept. 11, 2018.
  "Prometheus Unbound: Silence can't be bought" by Francis Gatuslao, *The Benildean*, Sept.
20, 2020.

REFERENCED BOOKS BY EILEEN R. TABIOS
  Prises (Double Take), trans. Fanny Garin (Angle Mort Editions, 2022)
  La Vie erotique de l'art, trans. Samuel Rochery, 2021 (Serie Discrete, 2021)

Because Poetry is a language for community, I am glad at the presence of so many poets in this book and thank them for expanding my poetry. Because this book focuses on poetic inventions, it doesn't mention the many other poets who have blessed my life with their lives and/or poems. I am grateful to all these poets, named and unnamed. —*Eileen R. Tabios*

Acknowledgments

Deep gratitude to the poets and visual artists worldwide who accepted and supported my poetry inventions and projects.

Salamat to Jose Tence Ruiz for creating the painting "Anghelpugay ng Kasarinlan (Elegiac Angel of Independence)," 1998 acrylic on canvas scroll (approx. 3' x 7') to commemorate the Centennial Anniversary of the Philippines' June 12, 1898 Declaration of Independence from Spain. Jose's painting was exhibited in one of my curated Centennial Anniversary poetry readings in New York. I saw it, snatched it, and brought it home where I lived with it for 25 years before I wrote its book. Salamat to the artist whose 3rd eye saw me.

I also thank Vince Gotera for naming the hay(na)ku; Mark Young, Jean Vengua, and Ernesto Priego for editing hay(na)ku anthologies; the poets who developed the hay(na)ku in its early days including the previously mentioned editors, Tom Beckett, John Bloomberg-Rissman, Aileen Cassinetto, Ivy Alvarez, William Allegrezza, Rebecca Mabanglo-Mayor, Glynda "Q-Tracer" Velasco, and lars palm; the poets mentioned in Chapter 2 for creating hay(na)ku variations; Ernesto Priego for authoring the first hay(na)ku book and introducing the form to comic strips; Jukka-Pekka Kervinen who published hay(na)ku books; Sheila E. Murphy, winner of Meritage Press' 2017-2018 Hay(na)ku Book Contest; Heikki Lahnaoja for the first Finnish hay(na)ku book; Radhey Shiam and his editor Rama Kant for the first hay(na)ku book in India; Dijana Petkova for the first two hay(na)ku books in Macedonia; Michelle Bautista who helped strengthen Meritage Press; those who taught hay(na)ku and MDR such as Melinda Luisa de Jesus, Michelle Bautista, Carol Dorf, Leny M. Strobel, and Malou Alorro; Rebeka Lembo who translated my hay(na)ku into Spanish and facilitated other hay(na)ku translations with members of the Poetry and Translation Seminar at the National Autonomous University of Mexico; the poets who supported MDR by writing its poems as noted in Chapter 3; Asian American Writers Workshop (AAWW), Eric Gamalinda who was then AAWW's Publications Director, and the BLACK LIGHTNING poets as noted in Chapter 4; Nick Carbo, strong advocate for Filipino literature; Summi Kaipa, the Alliance of Emerging Artists, Locus Arts Events Performance Space, Sonoma State University,

Leny M. Strobel, Barbara Jane Reyes, Michelle Bautista, Pusod Arts Gallery, *Interlope: A Journal of Asian America Poetics and Issues* for supporting my "Poem Tree" project; Holly Crawford and Anne Murray of AC Books who published my first novel *DOVELION*, a poetic novel; Napa Valley Poet Laureate Marianne Lyon and the Rotary Club of Napa for supporting the Flooid; Judge Philip Champlin (RIP) for writing the first Flooid poem; the first 20 poets to write Flooid poems as noted in Chapter 7; Thomas Fink for editing several of my prior poetry books; and all of the publishers of my books and chapbooks through which my inventions evolved and surfaced.

My thanks as well to Marsh Hawk Press, Managing Editor Sandy McIntosh for asking for this manuscript, then publishing it, as well as stellar book designer Mark Melnick. I am also grateful to Susan Terris and Gretchen Berger for reviewing/editing this book; Leny M. Strobel and Katrin de Guia whose works educated me on Kapwa, decolonialism and the indigenous Filipino which informed this book; Grace Talusan, Vicente L. Rafael, and Denise Low for their blurbed "advance words"; and the editors of the following publishers who previously published the following:

Closer to Liberation: Pin[a/x]y Activism In Theory and Practice, Editors Amanda Solomon Amorao, DJ Kuttin Kandi, and Jen Soriano (Cognella, San Diego, 2023): part of "Murder Death Resurrection" in Chapter 3.

Jacket2, Editor Divya Victor: part of "Murder Death Resurrection" in Chapter 3.

Chapter One: On Becoming a Poet, Editor Sandy McIntosh: the section on titling in Chapter 3.

Marsh Hawk Review, Editor Burt Kimmelman: the "Poem Tree" section of Chapter 3 and the "Poet's Novel" section of Chapter 4.

The following poems (some in earlier versions) appeared in my prior books:

"Kharkiv," "The Great Grief," and Judge Philip Champlin's "Good Works" in *Because I Love You, I Become War* (Marsh Hawk Press, 2023).

"My City of Baguio" in *The Thorn Rosary: Selected Prose Poems and New (1998-2010)* (Marsh Hawk Press, 2010).

"Grey, Surreptitiously" in *Reproductions of the Empty Flagpole* (Marsh Hawk Press, 2002).

"How Darkness Grows (Version 25)" in *MURDER DEATH RESURRECTION: A Poetry Generator* (Dos Madres Press, 2018).

Titles From Marsh Hawk Press

Jane Augustine *Arbor Vitae; Krazy; Night Lights; A Woman's Guide to Mountain Climbing*

Tom Beckett ~~Dipstick~~ *(Diptych)*

William Benton *Light on Water*

Sigman Byrd *Under the Wanderer's Star*

Patricia Carlin: *Original Green; Quantum Jitters; Second Nature*

Claudia Carlson *The Elephant House; My Chocolate Sarcophagus; Pocket Park*

Lorna Dee Cervantes: *April on Olympia*

Meredith Cole *Miniatures*

Jon Curley *Hybrid Moments; Scorch Marks; Remnant Halo*

Joanne D. Dwyer *RASA*

Neil de la Flor *Almost Dorothy; An Elephant's Memory of Blizzards*

Chard deNiord *Sharp Golden Thorn*

Sharon Dolin *Serious Pink*

Joanne Dominique Dwyer *Rasa*

Steve Fellner *Blind Date with Cavafy; The Weary World Rejoices*

Thomas Fink *Zeugma, Selected Poems & Poetic Series; Joyride; Peace Conference; Clarity and Other Poems; After Taxes; Gossip*

Thomas Fink and Maya D. Mason *A Pageant for Every Addiction*

Norman Finkelstein *Inside the Ghost Factory; Passing Over*

Edward Foster *A Looking-Glass for Traytors; The Beginning of Sorrows; Dire Straits; Mahrem: Things Men Should Do for Men; Sewing the Wind; What He Ought to Know*

Paolo Javier *The Feeling is Actual*

Burt Kimmelman *Abandoned Angel; Somehow; Steeple at Sunrise; Zero Point Poiesis; with Fred Caruso The Pond at Cape May Point*

Basil King *Disparate Beasts: Part Two; 77 Beasts; Disparate Beasts; Mirage; The Spoken Word / The Painted Hand from Learning to Draw / A History*

Martha King *Imperfect Fit*

David Lehman: *The Best of* The Best of

Phillip Lopate *At the End of the Day*

Mary Mackey *Breaking the Fever; The Jaguars That Prowl Our Dreams; Sugar Zone; Travelers With No Ticket Home; Creativity*

Jason McCall *Dear Hero*

Sandy McIntosh *The After-Death History of My Mother; Between Earth and Sky; Cemetery Chess; Ernesta, in the Style of the Flamenco; Forty-Nine Guaranteed Ways to Escape Death; A Hole In the Ocean; Lesser Lights; Obsessional; Plan B: Relational Elations of Orphaned Algebra*

Stephen Paul Miller *Any Lie You Tell Will Be the Truth; The Bee Flies in May; Fort Dad; Skinny Eighth Avenue; There's Only One God and You're Not It*

Daniel Morris *Blue Poles; Bryce Passage; Hit Play; If Not for the Courage*

Gail Newman *Blood Memory*

Geoffrey O'Brien *Where Did Poetry Come From; The Blue Hill*

Sharon Olinka *The Good City*

Christina Olivares *No Map of the Earth Includes Stars*

Justin Petropoulos *Eminent Domain*

Paul Pines *Charlotte Songs; Divine Madness; Gathering Sparks; Last Call at the Tin Palace*

Jacquelyn Pope *Watermark*

George Quasha *Things Done for Themselves*

Karin Randolph *Either She Was*

Rochelle Ratner *Balancing Acts; Ben Casey Days; House and Home*

Michael Rerick *In Ways Impossible to Fold*

Corrine Robins *Facing It; One Thousand Years; Today's Menu*

Eileen R. Tabios *The Inventor: A Poet's Transcolonial Autobiography; Because I Love You I Become War; The Connoisseur of Alleys; I Take Thee, English, for My Beloved; The In(ter)vention of the Hay(na)ku; Light Sang as It Left Your Eyes; Reproductions of the Empty Flagpole; Sun Stigmata; The Thorn Rosary*

Eileen R. Tabios and j/j hastain *The Relational Elations of Orphaned Algebra*

Tony Trigilio: *Proof Something Happened; Craft: A Memoir*

Susan Terris *Familiar Tense; Ghost of Yesterday; Natural Defenses; On Becoming a Poet* (editor)

Lynne Thompson *Fretwork*

Madeline Tiger *Birds of Sorrow and Joy*

Tana Jean Welch *Latest Volcano*

Harriet Zinnes: *Drawing on the Wall; Light Light or the Curvature of the Earth; New and Selected Poems; Weather is Whether; Whither Nonstopping*

YEAR	AUTHOR	TITLE	JUDGE
2004	Jacquelyn Pope	*Watermark*	Marie Ponsot
2005	Sigman Byrd	*Under the Wanderer's Star*	Gerald Stern
2006	Steve Fellner	*Blind Date with Cavafy*	Denise Duhamel
2007	Karin Randolph	*Either She Was*	David Shapiro
2008	Michael Rerick	*In Ways Impossible to Fold*	Thylias Moss
2009	Neil de la Flor	*Almost Dorothy*	Forrest Gander
2010	Justin Petropoulos	*Eminent Domain*	Anne Waldman
2011	Meredith Cole	*Miniatures*	Alicia Ostriker
2012	Jason McCall	*Dear Hero,*	Cornelius Eady
2013	Tom Beckett	~~Dipstick~~ *(Diptych)*	Charles Bernstein
2014	Christina Olivares	*No Map of the Earth Includes Stars*	Brenda Hillman
2015	Tana Jean Welch	*Latest Volcano*	Stephanie Strickland
2016	Robert Gibb	*After*	Mark Doty
2017	Geoffrey O'Brien	*The Blue Hill*	Meena Alexander
2018	Lynne Thompson	*Fretwork*	Jane Hirshfield
2019	Gail Newman	*Blood Memory*	Marge Piercy
2020	Tony Trigilio	*Proof Something Happened*	Susan Howe
2021	Joanne D. Dwyer	*Rasa*	David Lehman
2022	Brian Cochran	*Translation Zone*	John Yau
2023	Liane Strauss	*The Flaws in the Story*	Mary Jo Bang